A TALE OF TWO VISITS TO CHECHNYA

Book One
Grozny Visited 1939-40
Europe Ablaze
Bill Brison

Book Two
Grozny Revisited 1991
Revolution
Bill and Peggy Brison

A Tale of Two Visits to Chechnya
Bill and Peggy Brison
Available from
www.brisonbooks.co.uk
accepts credit cards Or send cheque to:
Bill and Peggy Brison
2 Scott Avenue, Bury, Lancs. BL9 9RS UK
Tel. 0161 764 3998
US $25 Canada $30 UK £13 Russia 660 Roubles

Published by Bill Brison

ISBN 0-9550730-0-6

Printed by Titus Wilson & Son, Kendal, Cumbria

Contents

Foreword v

Book One 1

Brison Family Journey to Grozny **1939-40 – Bill Brison**

My parents, Bill and Marion Brison, my younger brother, Davy and I (also called Bill Brison) went to Grozny, Chechnya, USSR in 1939 and returned in 1940. My youngest brother, Allan, was a baby and was left in the care of my mother's parents, Katie and Stanly Wilber. Grozny was a remote outpost of Imperial Russia. Besides being a great adventure, it was a defining moment for our family life. Allan came to feel a part of it. Mom wrote home to her small town newspaper, *The Allegany Citizen*, which reprinted her letters in full. *Life Magazine* gave extensive coverage. I was interested in going to Church, but was told the Church was closed. It wasn't closed, but it was dangerous for Russians to attend and only the most dedicated and brave went. I saw Grozny as a nine year old who played with the "street urchins" and had access to a Soviet society denied to American adults by Stalinist terror.

Life Magazine photographs 13

Marion Brison's letters 16

Chronology World War II 39

Book Two 40

Grozny Revisited **1991 – Bill and Peggy Brison**

In 1991, my wife, Peggy, and I returned to Grozny. We had the support and encouragement of the Archbishop of Canterbury, Robert Runcie. We spent two years arranging for the trip with the Moscow Patriarchate of the Russian Orthodox Church. One reason for this trip was nostalgia. The Holy Grail and more important factor was to find out if and how the Church of St. Michael and All Angels had survived 70 years of communist rule. We wanted to know more about the remarkable parish priest who served from 1917 to 1940 and who kept the Church open when churches all over the Soviet Union were closed and bulldozed. Incredibly, in 1991, we found a thriving and growing Church in the midst of yet another brutal war. We didn't find anything about that priest but found his re-incarnation in Fr. Piotr.

I   The Second Revolution 47

II   The Russian Orthodox Church in the Chechin Ingush Republic 56

III The University 69

IV   Walkabouts and Visits 71

V   Grozny Revisited – Reminiscences 77

     Chechnya Chronology 80

     The Sunday Times – May 15, 2005 81

     Acknowledgements 82

Dedication

Book One

To Dr. David Brison 1934-2002, my younger brother, Davy, in Book One. He shared in this first Chechnya visit. He encouraged me to write it up and contributed from his memories. We discussed the content of Book One. We had hoped he would see it in print.

Book Two

To Fr. Piotr, Parish Priest of St. Michael and All Angels, Grozny, Chechnya, saint and martyr. Peggy and I arrived in Grozny in 1991 to find him at the epicentre of a violet revolution in Grozny. He was the one person trusted alike by Muslims, Christians, atheists, communists, Russians, Chechins, and what was left of central government. His Church was booming. The demise of the communist state and ideology left a spiritual void with the people of Grozny hungering for a God they had denied existed. In the midst of this we arrived. But he found time to open his heart, his family, his Church, his city, and his people to us. He made us welcome and protected us.

When we returned to England, we heard he had been taken hostage and, like many others, presumed dead.

He had a heart condition but it was physical only. He was a brave and stout hearted servant of Christ.

Foreword

This book would be a simple tale of Grozny **visited** and **re-visited** except for a remarkable coincidence. In the long history of conflict between Russians and Chechins, there were just two years (1940 and 1991) in the 20th century where it was barely possible that with sensitive handling by Stalin, and then Yeltsin, the two races might have overcome their ancient divisions and lived "happily ever after" in a Muslim, Christian, Jewish Paradise. This didn't happen because each time, for different reasons, Soviet Russia came in with a heavy hand determined to eliminate the problem of Chechnya. History has shown that the only way this could have been done is by deporting or killing all the Chechins. Stalin tried, and Putin is trying (in 2005) to deport as many Chechins as he can. For over a century, Chechins have fought ferociously for their independence. This should have a familiar ring to Americans and British alike. In 1776-1812 Britain tried to suppress independence in the US colonies. A ragtag American army fought back Indian like by hiding behind trees and stone walls and firing at the overwhelming British force. George III retaliated (eventually) by burning Detroit and Washington D.C. Britain in the 19th, the U.S. in the 20th and now the US/UK in Iraq in the 21st are re-making the same error. What happened in Chechnya is happening in Iraq in 2005.

The author was in Chechnya in those two years (1940 and 1991) when there was reason to hope that a measure of Paradise might be possible.

The Brison family was in Chechnya in 1940 (Book One), Europe was ablaze (Chronology), Chechins were in the Red Army, a Chechin was Mayor of Grozny, Chechins and Russians bought and sold and socialized in the open market. It was possible to travel even in tribal areas. Soviet terror was rampant but applied to Russians as well as Chechins.

Assisted by the Archbishop of Canterbury, Bill and Peggy, his wife, went back to Grozny in 1991 (Book Two). The Holy Grail was to find out about the priest who held things together in 1917-1940. We arrived in the midst of another revolution. But still there were heart warming glimpses of Paradise. An Orthodox priest, Muslims, atheistic former communists, Chechins, and Russians shared power. We went on picnics in the country, were invited to give lectures and pray and both races were integrated in schools and university.

We found the Holy Grail, not in the priest of 1917, but in a priest of 1991,

Fr. Piotr, our friend and host and of blessed memory. He has since been taken hostage and presumed dead. Churches and Mosques alike have been destroyed in the Russian bombardment. Many of those who sheltered us (both Chechin and Russian) have died or left Grozny. Paradise lost.

This book shows that reconciliation even of ancient and bitter conflicts is possible. There can be a way other than "an eye for an eye". It is the way of the cross and "turning the other cheek", the only realistic basis of national policy as well as individual behaviour. In a David and Goliath confrontation, Mighty Russia, over decades with virtually unlimited resources in troops, modern weapons and with brutal disregard to the consequences to the civilian population have been unable to control or crush the Tiny Republic of Chechnya. This Book then has a lesson for 2005, particularly for that other David and Goliath situation, the war in Iraq, described by this Archbishop of Canterbury as "unjustified and unjustifiable". Even now, Paradise Regained is possible.

The author was ordained in the U.S. Episcopal Church. He has ancestors who sailed on the Mayflower and an Oneida Indian ancestor, whose cousins met the Mayflower. He was brought up on the Bill of Rights and the U.S. Constitution and matured with Martin Luther King. The Brison family immigrated to Britain in 1972 and Bill has served since then as a priest in the Church of England. He is the only person to have served as an Archdeacon in these two branches of the Anglican Communion. He and Peggy, his wife, a retired teacher, live in Bury, Lancs, UK.

Marion Brison finally succumbed to cancer at age 50. She and Bill lived for each other to the end. Bill (father), quit Max M. Miller and Co. when they dropped a research project to convert coal into a liquid fuel. He had an idea which would have worked; he died of a heart attack, aged 63. Davy (Dr. David Brison) died of pancreatic cancer, age 68, an early opponent of the attack on Iraq. Bill had a heart attack when he learned that the first Cruise missile had landed on a market in Baghdad. He and Peggy are now in good health. Paul Brison continues the family tradition of engineering going back to James, who worked for Edison. He is starting his own business in outdoor lighting based on his own patent. They have three other children: Daniel, Sarah and Martha.

Book One
Grozny Visited
1939-40
Europe Ablaze

An account of the visit of Bill Brison, Marion Wilber Brison with their sons, Billy (9) and Davy (4) to Grozny, Chechnya, written by Bill Brison (eldest son) and supplemented by Marion's letters.

My father was an oil engineer working for the firm of Max B. Miller. Engineering is in our blood. My great grandfather, James, worked as a janitor for Thomas Edison. He had been a hatter but developed a talent for blowing glass filaments. My grandfather, William, started as an roustabout on the oil rigs but became head chemist and second in command of Humble Oil, the predecessor of the Exxon behemoth, in spite of not having a high school education. Max B. Miller had patented a stage in the refining of oil. They were part of a consortium of American firms who had contracted with the Soviet government to construct an oil refinery in Grozny in southern Russia and to teach the Russians how to operate this refinery. My father was offered the chance of going to the USSR, as part of the Max B. Miller contingent. This was a great job opportunity and meant an important family decision, because he wouldn't go without us. I was 9, my brother David, 4, and we had a younger brother, Allan, who was a baby. Our parents consulted with my mother's parents who agreed to take care of Allan for the time we would be gone. They were concerned about my education and went to see the School Principal, Mr. Stuart Race. He was very supportive, saying that, "educationally, it would be the best year of his life." How did the Principal of a small primary school in Glen Rock, N. J. have that kind of insight? Our mother was a Kindergarten teacher and David's schooling was not a problem. The political situation in Europe must have been a problem. The Germans were measuring Jews' noses on the street and had confiscated all Jewish property. Hitler went into Austria in 1938 and into Prague on March 15th, 1939, as we were getting ready to go.

Incredibly, we went anyway, setting sail from New York City to London on

Billy and David Brison on the American Banker on the way to Chechnya.

the American Banker, a small freighter which carried a few passengers. None of us had been outside the US before. My parents were both brought up in rural upstate New York. We passed the Statue of Liberty and out across the Atlantic. The American Banker had a great bonus for small boys. It carried zoo animals in the hold. In the mornings, a giraffe stuck his head up the hatch. I went out to look and a chimpanzee came to join me, sitting beside me on the hatch and putting his arm companionably across my shoulders. He was smelly and I wasn't too pleased but was ashamed to admit it since the sailors thought it was hilarious. Mom dashed out to the rescue and the sailors thought that was even funnier. I protested manfully but was secretly relieved. Our great aunt Julia, who was a spinster school teacher in Paterson, New Jersey, and not, I would have thought, that kind of a person, had done a thoughtful thing. She had individually wrapped up a gift for me and Davy for each day we were aboard ship. They were simple: games, a small penknife, puzzles, pencils and drawing equipment. How we looked forward to opening those gifts! We stayed in London a few days before setting sail again. Pop was most impressed in London by the pipe towel racks which served the dual purpose of heating the rooms and drying the towels. Our central heating in Glen Rock was a coal burning furnace in the basement which had to be fired up every morning. Pop later got several patents and was always intrigued by such applications. We got to Moscow via the Kiel Canal, the Baltic Sea and Leningrad. Our boat was so close to the shore in the Kiel Canal that we could almost reach out and pat the cows. The pastoral scene was in stark contrast to what was going on elsewhere in Germany. Smells evoke memories. Sixty years later, whenever I smell the smell that comes from stainless steel containers that are used to keep food hot, I recall the Leningrad hotel where I first smelled that smell.

Moscow was turbulent. Mom and I went to Lenin's Tomb in Red Square. There were long lines of people wanting to go through the tomb to see the body and kiss the glass coffin over his forehead. I waited in line. Mom wanted to take an outside photo of the tomb and the Kremlin wall. The Red Army guard shook his head. Mom, thinking she had misunderstood started to focus. The guard raised his rifle and pointed it at us. We heard a metallic click. Mom put the camera away quickly. She was very shaken.

For some reason, I was playing with the British Ambassador's son. A Russian butler was caught making a recording in the attic of the Embassy of confidential

Lenin's Tomb.

3

ambassadorial conversations. The British were upset. It just went to show what cads the communists were. No sense of etiquette! We would never do a thing like that! This was, of course, primitive in the light of the sophisticated electronic surveillance that was developed later by the British and all countries. We were in Moscow when von Ribbentrop and Molotov signed a Non-Aggression Pact and Stalin proposed a toast to the Fuhrer. The British, led by my playmate's father, had been carrying on negotiations of their own to enlist Russia in a pact aimed at discouraging German aggression in Poland. These negotiations had reached a sensitive stage, and the British had been deceived into believing that the Russians were almost ready to agree, when the Soviets signed with the Nazis. The British were wrong footed and furious. This made WW2 virtually inevitable. Nonetheless, we stayed on and, after checking with the US Embassy, we made plans to go to Grozny. This wasn't easy. The Russians had every reason to get my father to Grozny quickly so that the refinery could start producing as soon as possible. Pop would go off daily to pick up our train tickets. We had been strongly advised only to go first class. He would be given third class, then second, class. Day after day this went on. I ate some coffee ice cream in the hotel and was violently sick. We finally got the first class tickets after days of frustration. Apparently it wasn't just availability. It was the kind of thing the Soviets liked to do to show that in a classless society we are all equal. There was some justification for their behaving this way. The Americans and British didn't think much of the Russians and were arrogant in their dealings with Russians. We soon found out the necessity of first class tickets. I was permitted to wander down the coaches on the train down to Grozny. Third class were just cattle cars, no seats or bunks, people jammed in sitting or lying on the floors. Second class had some board bunks which one person could lie on but there was no privacy, the whole coach was open. In first class, we had compartments and bunks. The Russians considered Davy and me novelties, especially when they realized we didn't speak Russian and were Americanskis. There was a Russian woman with large breasts nursing her baby and people singing and arguing. It broke up the monotony of the long journey and I picked up a bit of Russian.

We arrived in Grozny to be greeted at the railroad station by the 5 or 6 American families already there. Yasha, an interpreter assigned to the Americans, was there playing the accordian. Mom burst into tears when she saw our apartment. We were in what was for the Russians a luxury apartment block and moved into the one recently and hurriedly vacated by an American who had struck a Russian refinery worker. Our flat was on the second floor. A wood stove provided heat, cooking and hot water for baths. This didn't bother my

Grozny American Group Life Magazine *Photo.*

mother. Her mother cooked all her life on a wood stove in upstate New York . . . Bringing the wood up two flights of stairs could have been a problem but it turned out that it was delivered. It was just the dreariness of it all. Mom had cancer, had had one breast removed and wasn't feeling too well. The floors were covered in torn linoleum and the walls were bare. We were assigned a maid, Maria, who turned out to be a very fine person, good humored and hard working. We learned later that the maids weren't provided for our comfort. They were there to spy on us. She started the fires and did part of the cooking. Things began to look up. We had three rooms, one of which Davy and I shared, another was our parents' bedroom and we used the third as a living room. There was no TV, of course, only radio in Russian and the BBC Overseas Service once a day. Otherwise, nothing but a loudspeaker on a pole outside the apartment blaring out Russian music and propaganda 24 hours a day. We were in a strange land and didn't speak Russian so we spent a lot of time in that room. Russian adults, including other families in the apartment block, wouldn't speak to the Americans The secret police were everywhere and they were frightened to be seen even talking with an American adult. In addition to the three rooms we had a kitchen and a bathroom. This accommodation was shared by 3 Russian families, a family in each room and they shared the kitchen and bathroom. They considered themselves very lucky to have this.

Brison's Apartment Building ⟵ indicates their Flat.

Home Schooling

It was decided that I wouldn't go to the Russian school. The other Americans didn't send their children because they didn't think the school was any good and I didn't speak enough Russian to understand the lessons. In England and America immigrant children from all over go to regular schools with no knowledge of English and seem to do amazingly well. My wife is a teacher and has taught all kinds. My parents had been given some 5th grade school books

Housing near Brison Flat 1939.

with the intention of covering what I would have been doing at home. This didn't last very long. First Mom and then Pop tried it. They had brought along my Encyclopedia Britannica Junior, which I had loved browsing through at home. But Russian Customs in Leningrad had taken this to see whether there was subversive information in it. They said they would return it but months went by. Pop protested vigorously. It seemed just another Russian way of putting us in our place. It finally arrived only months before we left and then it had articles and even pages cut out, anything to do with German or Russian history, Lenin, Stalin or his new found friend, Hitler. In any case, I found the outside world far more interesting than studying.

Outdoor Education: The Market

When we first arrived in Grozny, we stayed close to home. But Maria took us to the market which was in easy walking distance. We were told it was the only open, free market in the Soviet Union. Peggy and I found the market and our apartment house when we returned in 1991. The Chechen would bring their produce down from the hills. We didn't buy meat there. The Americans were assigned a man, Jon, whose job it was to procure meat and anything else we wanted. Jon was a tall, pleasant, Lithuanian, who used to come and go mysteriously. He was a free spirit in a land where most were frightened conformists. My father had grown up on a farm and suspected the meat was horse meat. We used to welcome his visits, not only for what he brought but also for news of the Russian world. On the market, women would sell milk in pitchers and would ladle it into containers which we brought. The milk had to be well boiled. This must have been difficult on a wood stove and sometimes it tasted burned. I haven't been able to stand boiled milk since. Russian women, sometimes men, would sit on the ground with a few, pathetic trinkets for sale spread out on the ground before them. Sometimes there were things Mom was interested in, a brass tray, a pewter pitcher, etc. After a while and after earnest and incessant pleading, my Mom would let me go alone, or with Russian friends, at first just to buy fruit and vegetables. Sometimes I would spot something I thought she would like, e.g. a brass samovar or a Chechin knife or sword. The swords were short, the same size and shape as the Roman sword, with intricately worked silver scabbards. These were probably family heirlooms and I have since regretted getting them. When I spotted something, I would sprint home, tell Mom and she would give me roubles to buy it. Pop was given an allowance in roubles which couldn't be exchanged for any other currency. We weren't allowed to travel. This meant we had a lot of money which could only be spent on such things. So I would get my roubles, dash to the market and haggle with the Russians or Chechins. We picked up a couple of brass samovars this way. One time I spotted a grizzled old Chechin with a sword. I came back with what must have been for him a King's ransom. He seemed a bit bemused by this little American kid with all this money, but he was quite willing to sell his sword. As we haggled, we collected quite a crowd, including a bunch of boys who hung around the market, some of whom I knew and played with. They were kids about my age who has run away from home, escaped from state homes or were playing hooky from school. They were a rough lot who slept out

Grozny Market.

in all weather and lived off their wits, generally by stealing in the market or from homes. Naturally, they were interested in me and my wad of cash. They pressed in close and this made me highly uneasy. There was a Red Army policeman watching. But I knew that he wouldn't be any help. The Chechin and I agreed on a price and I peeled off the bills and gave it to him. I took the rest and started to put them in my back pocket. I realized that wasn't smart because of the gang. The money was gone before I got my hand back to my pocket. I turned and looked accusingly at the kid behind me. He turned his pockets out to show me he hadn't done it. As I looked down the row of kids each turned his pockets out, daring me to do anything about it. The policeman turned away (a rich American kid vs. these ragamuffins?) There was no way I could find the money. So I headed home with my sword.

In the year we were there oranges appeared on the market twice. There was no warning. All of a sudden they were there. The word went around and they were gone in an hour or two. Because I was on the streets I found out right away and got first in the queue. One time I went and had worked my way up to the stall when I saw a grubby hand creep up and enclose an orange. On impulse I grabbed his wrist and held on tightly. I told the stall owner who just gave me a withering look. Go away American kid and stop bothering me. The thief was one of my street friends.

Outside Education: Russian and Chechin Friends

Russian or Chechin adults were too frightened of the secret police to talk with American adults, even on the street. But the children of both races would talk with me and I had a gang of friends. Russian parents worked a long day. The mothers would leave early in the morning, give their kids a chunk of black bread, which was their food for the day, and the kids were more or less free to do what they wanted. The kids taught me Russian and I taught them some "English?" As in when we chose up sides, eenie, meenie, minie, mow catch a nigger by the toe, if he hollers let him go, eenie, meenie, mini mow, my mother says to choose this one" I knew "nigger" wasn't right but I didn't know how to alter it so that we could choose sides. And, after all, that's what we said in Glen Rock N. J.! Then they wanted to know what a "nigger" was and were astounded when I told them it was a black or brown person. They had never heard of such a person. They wanted to know whether they had faces like we did and what language they spoke. There is a rule among politicians that when you are in a hole, stop digging. I couldn't stop because they were so fascinated by the whole idea. I just hoped they'd forget the word and I'd substitute, "negro" next time. We generally played hide n seek type games or went to the market.

We were in a large compound, with the apartments around the sides. Many of us had dogs and when another dog would stray into "our" compound, we would take off like gangbusters and, hooting and hollering, chase it with our dogs. This was not a great macho event. Dog fights are usually just a pretence of growling, snarling and snapping. After some of this being egged on by us, the errant dog would roll over on his back and whine. My dog, "Boots", was particularly unaggressive, much to my chagrin. No amount of urging would get Boots to do anything more than curl his lip a little. We had one dog that wasn't ours but used to come along for the chase. We called her "Ma" because she always seemed to have a litter of puppies. She was a little, terrier type and she would have a go. Even so, it never amounted to anything. Ma lived in a compound near our flat. In the same compound there was a big pig which we used to ride. It would squeal and jump around and we had a good time. My father told me it could be dangerous and to stay away so I did, for a while.

The Secret Police NKVD

The KGB, or NKVD as they were then known, were omnipresent and the people in Grozny lived in constant fear. It didn't take much,or anything, to get their unwelcome attention. Going to Church was out for all but a handful of old ladies. St. Michael and All Angels was open, unusual in Russia at that time. It was thriving when we went back in 1991. But in 1940, it was a sad affair. NKVD were there at service times to take attendance. If you went to Church you could lose your job, your children could be denied education, and you were more likely to be sent to the Gulag. So nobody but the very brave went to Church. Icons in homes were not forbidden but it was dangerous to have them and they were hidden well away. In their place of honour in the home were pictures of Lenin and Stalin. This was not mandatory but then any good Soviet citizen would be proud to have these in his home. If the NKVD investigated, it counted against you if you didn't have the portraits of Stalin and Lenin.

Maria, our maid, let us know that she and the other maids were interrogated twice a week. She asked us not to reveal our source of this information. We weren't doing anything we needed to hide and we were there working for the Soviet government. The information that we were, in effect, being spied on made us more cautious in our relationships with Russians. Yasha, the interpreter, would listen to the BBC Overseas Service with the American men each evening. They met in the apartment where there was the best radio. A lot was going on. Poland and Finland were invaded. One night the maid in that flat made the pretext that she had left something behind and came back. They turned off the radio but Yasha was there with the American men. They must have put two and two together. In any case the mere suspicion was enough. Yasha was gone the next morning. We made frantic enquiries. We were told by Jon or Maria that he was probably OK because they needed interpreters. But Stalin had decimated the Soviet Officer Corps, his own inner circle, put millions including priests, nuns, doctors and other professions which were needed by the nation into concentration camps. Would he stop at one interpreter? We never heard from him or about him. He was a valued friend.

As a boy I was well aware of the prevalent terror. I had a Mickey Mouse watch which was the envy of my friends. One of them offered to buy it. This was a little strange since most of them had so little money. I didn't want to sell it but he finally offered me the equivalent in roubles of $32. It had cost me £1 in the US. I agreed and he wanted me to go to his house to show it to his parents. I knew I shouldn't do that, not for my sake, but it could be dangerous for his family. I checked with Pop who said absolutely not. I went back to the boy and he checked with his father and said there would be no problem ("nitchevoo" literally "no problem"). We went back and forth many times before I went to his home, showed his parents the watch and sold it to him. The only way that family could have risked my visit was if one or both of the parents were high in the NKVD.

One other home I was in, although I don't remember it, was the home of the communist Mayor of Grozny. His daughter told me in 1991 that the knock came at the door in the middle of the night and he was taken away. They didn't see him or hear of him for two years. Terror was everywhere. There were no reasons or explanations made. The family just had to assume he was guilty of some terrible crime. One of the American kids came to the door the next morning and asked what the father had done. This made it hard on the family. Everyone assumed he was a criminal. The family were shunned. The random nature of the terror made it worse.

While we were there, the Director of the refinery was replaced and then his successor replaced. One day he was there, fully in charge of the whole works, the next morning he was gone. When they arrived for work, the American men asked to see the Director by name but none of the workers even knew who they were talking about. A new Director was there and so they dealt with him. The Russian workers were so afraid that the former Director's name was never mentioned again.

Finland

The Russians invaded Finland on Nov. 30th, 1939. They won great victories and we heard martial music over the loud speaker. In spite of the victories, each day the front line moved nearer Russia. Ill equipped Russian troops were invading a nation fighting for its life. The Finns' forces were well equipped and included ski troops. They clobbered the Russians, inflicting a humiliating defeat. Many Russians were killed, wounded or frostbitten. To conceal the wounded, the Russians sent some of them to the hospital in Grozny. An American girl ("Billy" Morris) and I were curious. We went to the hospital, asked at the front door if we could visit. We were told off. Even the soldiers' relatives weren't told they were there and if they found out weren't allowed to visit.

We snuck around to a back door and, sure enough, there, in a ward, were all these wounded men. They seemed happy to see us, probably we were a welcome diversion, and we chatted for sometime. My Russian was good enough by then so that they probably didn't realize we were Americans. One of the men seemed suspicious, they began to talk and we left hurriedly. Pop was not pleased! Who knows what the Soviets would have done if we had been caught? Stalin had no reason to make concessions to Americans.

Leaving

The war news got worse and worse. The US Ambassador came all the way down to see us. The time had come to leave, in fact it was nearly too late. There were two possibilities, one was the trans Siberian railroad to Japan. Thankfully we didn't take that route or we might have been interred in Japanese prison camps. Instead we elected to go out through Turkey and on to Greece, and Italy. It was a tense time. The Nazis were everywhere victorious and Italy was an ally. I can't imagine why we were permitted to go to the USSR or why we stayed so long, a small group of Americans alone in a remote area of southern Russia. I said goodbye to my Russian friends and we said a tearful goodbye to Maria, who had been such a good friend. Mom asked if it would be safe for her to write and Maria said yes. She wrote a couple of letters but came to the conclusion that it was dangerous for Maria. We never heard from her again. I hoped I might find her in 1991 but I didn't.

Luggage Label.

We set sail on the Conte Savoia, the last ocean liner to leave Italy for the US.

When the boat docked my mother got the tragic news that Grandma Wilber had been injured in a car crash while coming to meet the boat. She was able to talk with us but died in hospital a few days later.

When we got home we found we were famous, at least in our small town of Glen Rock, N. J. *Life Magazine*, the coffee table magazine of choice at the time had given a large spread to the American group. I went to what remained of the Fifth Grade year and was asked to make the round of the other classes, telling of my adventures, showing my Chechin swords and other artefacts.

The End of Book One

Alexander Willis, dressed for a party in a hillsman's *shapka* and with a Dagestan knife in his teeth, poses before a mantel which supports Ferdinand (*left*) and Dopey (*right*).

His wife Mildred did her marketing at Grozny in the public bazaar. A vender with the itch sells dried apples and apricots and fresh pears at 60¢ a pound. Wine is plentiful.

Russian Album

After almost two years in U.S.S.R. an American engineer returns with these revealing photos

New pictures from Russia are as rare as a 1913 Liberty-head nickel. Sovfoto, the official picture agency, releases precious few. During the Finnish war only a handful reached the U. S. from the Soviet side. Across this Red barrier recently came these informal photographs taken by Alexander Willis, an American in charge of an aviation oil refinery at Grozny, capital of the Chechen Republic near the Caspian Sea.

Engineer Willis left Russia in May after a stay of almost two years. His report: Grozny's 170,000 people were better fed, better dressed than when he had seen them once before in 1932; housing had improved but was still cramped; "t.b." and typhoid were prevalent; despite all Soviet attempts to speed up production, the Russian worker is as disinterested and sluggish as ever.

THESE AMERICANS REPRESENT GROZNY'S ENTIRE FOREIGN POPULATION

WILLIS LIVED IN CITY'S BEST APARTMENT WHICH TOOK 42 MONTHS TO BUILD

OIL TRUST GAVE WILLIS HIS RUSSIAN-BUILT "ZIS" WITH BUICK ENGINE

MARUSSA, THE MAID, SPENT HER MONEY IN GROZNY'S FIRST BEAUTY PARLOR

CONTINUED ON NEXT PAGE 73

Life Magazine *Article.*

Community swimming pool is a cement basin, 40 by 125 ft., which has chlorinated water. Swimmers bunch together in the warm water flowing into pool from the pipe.

At the water "automat" at Makhach-Kala, capital of nearby Dagestan, women put the equivalent of 4¢ in a slot and pump out a pailful. City dwellers pay water rent.

The speculators' section in the market place at Grozny is where poorest element buys and sells old clothes and junk at a profit. License to speculate here costs one ruble.

A Cossack and a Chechen carpenter talk things over on a Grozny side street. The Cossack wears traditional dress and the carpenter has on a typical padded cotton suit.

This shepherd from the hills visits the bazaar at Grozny. The black cape he wears is made of felt. Cap is sheepskin. Even on hot summer days he dresses this warmly.

Life Magazine *Article.*

14

Grozny's trams were always jammed. Theater in rear, decorated with portraits of Molotov, Lenin, Stalin, Voroshilov, gives plays. City has several movie houses.

Carrying Red banners the union leaders of Grozny led May Day parade outside the Willis' apartment in 1939. White-bloused militia in background are ordinary police.

People danced fox trots in streets of Grozny on May Day 1939 to an accordion that played tunes from two-year-old American movies. In summer people dance in park.

Son of the president of Chechen Republic lived in same apartment house as Willis. Windows of building were boarded up awaiting the tardy arrival of glass panes.

Willis saw 1940 Moscow May Day parade from window of U. S. Embassy. Red Square is in the background, a corner of Kremlin at right. The building at left is old Duma.

Life Magazine *Article.*

July 14th

We are off! After all the planning and buying and packing at last we can relax. Harold MacShaw brought us to the boat and after all the baggage was checked and details seen to we walked over the gang plank onto the boat. Our state room is small - hardly room for all our baggage and four of us. People began to come - Mrs Tilghman, Clara Swienstra, Sally and Arthur, Lois Reick, Jr. & Buddy, Dot & Wes Case, Tod & Gladys Fisher, Bobsy & Billy, Elizabeth Jamison & men from the office. Finally the gong sounded for everybody to leave. Everybody waved & waved and at last the boat pulled out.

Billy & David could hardly wait to get into the stateroom and up into the upper berth. There they stayed reading the funnies that Billy Fisher gave them and climbing up and down the ladder. At

Marion Brison's first letter home describing the ship.
July 14th, 1939.

least Billy climbed up and down. David could only climb up so every few minutes Billy would come running for Daddy to lift David down. At six o'clock the dinner gong sounded and we went down to the dining room and all ate a good dinner, which I lost immediately upon coming up stairs. From then on I lay on my bunk not caring much about anything and wishing I was back on land.

The Bathroom steward came to arrange for our shower baths and the room steward kept coming in to do anything he could to make us comfortable.

The children and Bill slept fine all night – me not so good – and we were all awake at five-thirty.

July 15th

Everybody went down to breakfast but me and all day I lay around enjoying the miseries of sea sickness

Marion Brison's first letter – continued.

17

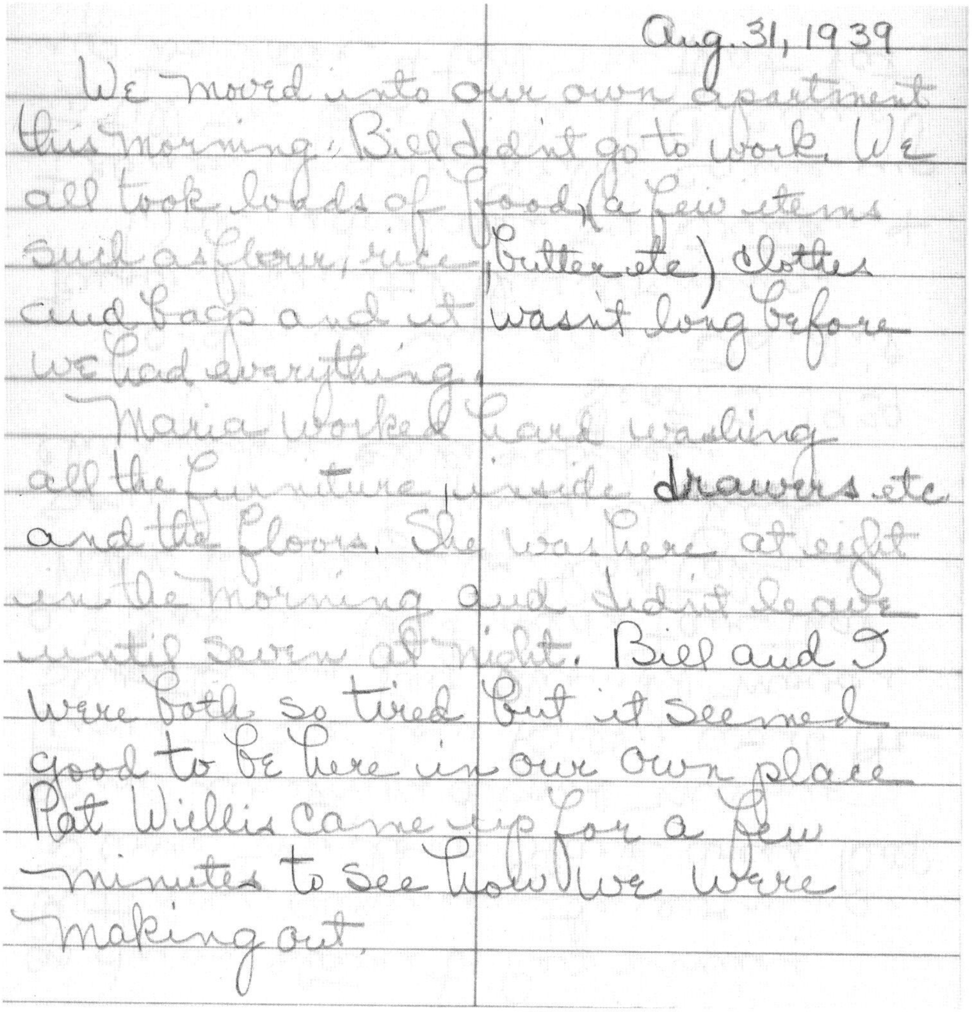

Aug. 31, 1939

We moved into our own apartment this morning. Bill didn't go to work. We all took loads of food (a few items such as flour, rice, butter, etc.) clothes and bags and it wasn't long before we had everything.

Maria worked hard washing all the furniture, inside drawers etc and the floors. She was here at eight in the morning and didn't leave until seven at night. Bill and I were both so tired but it seemed good to be here in our own place. Pat Willis came up for a few minutes to see how we were making out.

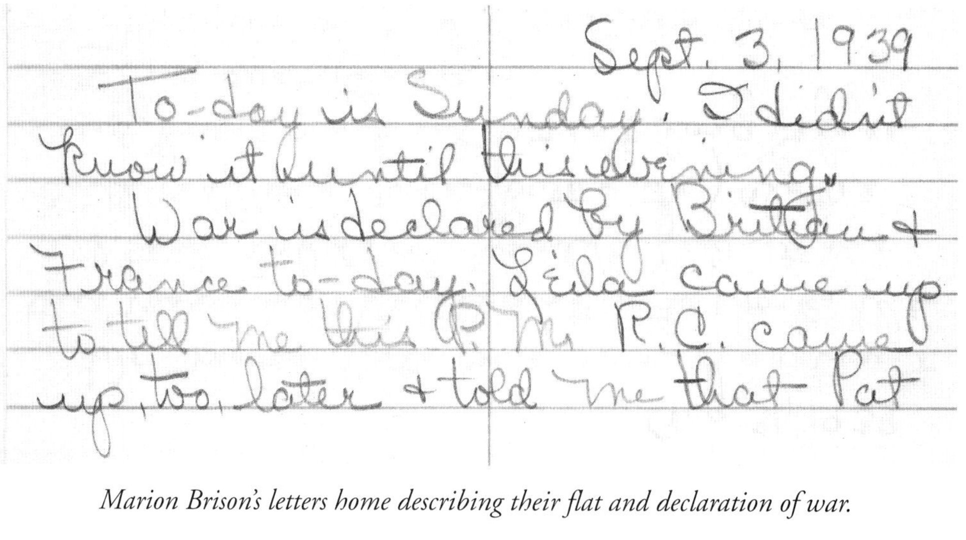

Sept. 3, 1939

To-day is Sunday. I didn't know it until this evening.

War is declared by Brittain + France to-day. Leila came up to tell me this P. M. R. C. came up, too, later + told me that Pat

Marion Brison's letters home describing their flat and declaration of war.

Rest Day - Sept 12,

Rest day was an uneventful one for us altho some of the Americans had quite some excitement. Bill & I went to the market & looked around in the junk market but didn't see anything we wanted to buy. We came home and I started dinner. R.C. came in about noon to tell us that Pat, Bruce & Faith had been arrested for taking pictures over in the market. They were held there about two hours & a half & finally released but not given back their cameras.

After our dinner we went over to Midlums (not home) and then to Hackstaffs to hear all about the experience. Ed, & Agnes Pat, the Morrises, & Dan & Mary went out to the place where they ride the horses. We took a walk over across the river to the dish store

Marion Brison's letter home describing market visits.

& bought 4 compote dishes & salt & pepper shakers. Our Baggage came! We got one of our boxes up & emptied.

WEd. Sept 13

Billy & David went to market with Mary J. I heard all about yesterday. Mary J looked around the junk market but didn't find anything we could want. I bought some fine salt (which can't be gotten all the time) & some little hand cut wooden paddles 45 kopeks each.

The baggage was still in the store room in the other apt but we opened one of our boxes down there & we all carried stuff up. Billy & David helped a lot, Bruce helped Bill carry up the one box of electrical things & we got those things out. How good it seems to have things from home! 18 jars of peanut butter, 4 cans of ham, chipped beef, corned beef, coffee & oats!

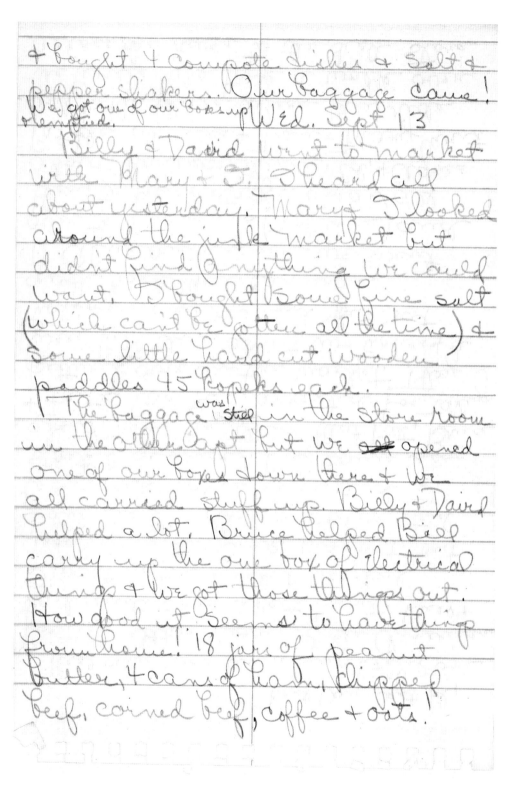

Marion Brison's letter home – arrival of their baggage.

20

Milk 40¢ Per Quart And Eggs At $1.50 Per Dozen In Russia

Such Is The Experience of Mrs. Marion Wilber Brison According To Another Interesting Letter Received By Her Parents in Allegany.

The following is another very interesting letter from Mrs. Marion Wilber Brison who with her husband is living in Russia. The letter is addressed to her parents, Mr. and Mrs. Stanley P. Wilber of this village:

September 19, 1939

Dearest Family.

We are all settled and into the routine of things here now and getting along very nicely. I told you about our apartments. Ours is very pleasant since we have our own things around. I have the enlarged family picture over the buffet here in the living room where I can see it all the time. We have a book case with our encyclopedia on it besides "Reaching for the Stars" and the story books. We were furnished with strips of carpeting, which I sewed together one night for a living room rug. The wood stove in the kitchen is a joy. I never knew I could enjoy a wood stove. It is built right up against the wall, of cement and covered with white calcimine. We have dry wood brought to us as often as the wood box gets empty and it is next to nothing to get a fire started. We have two electric hot plates and an electric heated aluminum kettle. It has the heating element inside. The hot plates are on a table by themselves. We have quite a big square table in the kitchen besides a dish cabinet and a sink.

I was discouraged about the bathroom when I first saw it. It is a big room, painted a dark grey. It had an ugly dark colored tub in it, but that was removed and a white one put in it. The wood box is in there—and the ice box! Bill asked one day if I had told you that our ice box is in the bathroom. It has to be there because the water drains onto the floor (it needs repairing.) Nevertheless, it is a little inconvenient at times having to wait to get into the icebox when dinner is in the making. I fixed up the looks of the place a little by putting a strip of carpet down in there and putting the garbage pail and scrubbing pail, clothesline and pins, etc., into a box turned on its side which I am making a curtain to cover.

The electricity was off for thirty-six hours—went off at 6:30 A. M. the morning of the 17th. We usually use the hot plates for breakfast but had to build a wood fire in a hurry. Night came and we ate by candlelight. Billy and David thought it was fun, of course. They went to bed early and we all listened to the victrola for awhile before they went to sleep. Dot and Wes Case lent us that victrola and the boys have had so much fun with it. Bruce and Faith came over in the evening to sit by candlelight with us. We had three little candles on the table and were playing bridge when there was a knock at the door. Reg, Lilah and R. C. Smith joined our circle around the table. Another knock and that time it was Pat Willis (boss of the job) and Mr. Rastmussen. It was fun. We had no light all day yesterday until last night at six o'clock.

Bill has to be at work at 7:30 A. M. He takes a lunch and gets home at five or sometimes later. A car stops for the men and brings them home. This lunch business is on my mind a lot—I never had that experience. I never did so much baking. I make apple pies, white cakes, and chocolate cakes, oatmeal cookies and peanut butter cookies. Bill take four or five sandwiches, a tomato, usually and cake or cookies. He makes tea over at the lab.

Our big thought here is food. Every morning we go to market. Mary stops for me about nine. The market is a big open place with open stalls where the people sell their fruit. vegetables (string beans, tomatoes, potatoes, egg plant, celery and every vegetable you could think of), milk and cream, eggs, flowers. Billy and David always go along and each carry a basket. This morning we got carrots, peppers and string beans, apples for sauce, and walnuts for cook-

Marion Brison's letter to her parents describing their daily life. Reprinted in "The Allegany Citizen".

ples for sauce, and walnuts for cookies, and eggs. A woman brings over milk to the door every day. I buy three liters which is about 3½ quarts. It is 2 rubles (40c) a liter. A woman comes to us with chickens. I got one today for 15 rubles ($3.00). We never ate so many chickens—sometimes two a week. Chickens and eggs are plentiful but other meat isn't so easy to get. One day we had a beef roast. The eggs are 6½ rubles ($1.30) for 10. When we go to market we always visit the free market first. The people there don't have to pay for ther spot to sell their goods. There they have everything imaginable laid out on the ground—old key rings and keys, old shoes, radio parts, lamps and once in a while something nice. I found a brass pitcher one day which is the envy of all the Americans. Then a few days later I found a brass tray. I paid 23 rubles for the pitcher and 15 rubles for the tray. They aren't dented like some things are. There are usually teams of oxen and covered wagons, teams of water buffalo and once in a while a team of camels. David hasn't seen the camels yet and every morning we look for them. This morning, just as we were leaving the market. a herd (or is it a flock?) of about 50 pigs were being driven down the road.

After we came home from market Billy starts his school work and I get the milk boiled, cooled and in pitchers in the icebox, water too. I help Billy with his work and lunch time comes before we know it. People are in and out all day. Maybe somebody gets a bit of news on the radio and everybody must know, or somebody else needs an egg for a cake or somebody else just wants to talk.

Maria is our maid and is a woman about 50, very pleasant and a good hard worker. She walk around here in bare feet or stocking feet. She comes early, about eight. eats her breakfast and then begins her work. This A. M. she washed. It is a long process all done by hand but by two o'clock she was hanging out the clothes. She takes up the rugs every other day and washes up the floor. She always removes any foot gear she might have on for that. She builds the fire if it is necessary, fixes all the vegetables. She is very interested in any Americansky (that is what we are called here) stuff especially the knitting. She loves to sew and has hemed the carpet strips. One day she was sitting in the hall on the floor with her bare feet out in front of her and I said to Agnes Midlum who was here: "If my mother could see that!"

Maria and I have a great time with our sign language but get along fine. She loves the boys, too, and talks her Russian to them.

We are the largest group of Americans in Russia on business. The American Embassy in Moscow is in touch with us all the time and should it become necessary to leave we will be taken care of. The Embassy said yesterday by phone that we are safe here. We know there is a war but hear nothing except once in a while a little on the radio. Don't worry about us.

Give everybody our love.

Marion

Marion's letter to parents – continued.

Davy, Bill and Billy Brison, R.C. Smith on a trip out.

Scene on a country trip out.

October 22, 1939

Dear Folks:

Another Sunday! We go from rest day to rest day and the days of the week are forgotten. Rest days are the 6th, 12th, 18th, 24th, and 30th days of every month.

Last rest day was a big one for us. By some miracle Pat was able to get a bus and driver. When one thinks he would like a ride around here, he just keeps on wishing he could have a ride. Cars aren't for hire. The Smiths have been here a year and have never been outside Grozny until we took our trip.

Well, anyway after much talking and letter writing by Pat, he was promised a bus driver on rest day October 18th. Even then he couldn't be sure of it until he saw it in front of the apartment. Well, it was there at ten o'clock in the morning.

I cooked a chicken that night before for sandwiches, made hot chocolate for the thermos, and had half a chocolate cake, and made cinnamon buns that morning. We were the first ones down to the bus. We had been told to dress warmly because we were going to the mountains so we had plenty of coats, etc.

It was a beautiful, sunshiny, clear day. There were the Smiths, Lilah, Reg. and R. C., Mr. and Mrs. Morris and Billy, Bruce and Faith Hackstaff, Ed., and Agnes Midlum and Betsy, Pat Willis, Rassie, Jean Petrovish and his son (the Russian who looks after the American needs) and us Brisons. Dan Volkmar was sick with a cold so he and Mary gave up the trip at the last minute.

The road we took outside of Grozny wasn't a lovely paved highway (there aren't such things here) but a good dirt road. We went on and on up into the foot hills of the Caucasus Mountains.

Every little while we stopped to let every one pile out to take pictures. The mountains were beautiful. Once there was an oil derrick which evidently was supposed to be moved but *had been* left in the middle of the road. We held our breaths while we went around that.

Another time we came to a stream with no bridge. We stopped and waited while four or five teams of water buffalo forded the stream, and then we drove through. It had a hard rock bottom.

Another time we came upon a big herd of goats--white ones, black ones, brown, and black and white. They went right up the side of a mountain so fast when our bus came along.

Marion Brison's letter home describing the trip out into the countryside.

Finally we came to the place Jean had in mind for us to stop near a sanitarium--a beautiful place all landscaped. We were much more interested in the Che-chins who lived in their huts near here.

The Che-chins are the people who live in this section of Russia. They are an obscure race of Mohammendan extraction. Most of the men have three wives. One day, one of the engineers saw a Che-chin walking down the street with his three wives behind him. He came to a puddle and waited,-and his three wives carried him across.

The Che-chin men gathered around, or rather we surrounded them trying to bargain for their knives. A poor Che-chin woman was so pleased to have her picture taken. They all carry knives about 15 inches in length and wear their rags with proud dignity. Evidently these Che-chins were prosperous because they wouldn't sell.

One Che-chin did a prayer for us--starting first by removing his boots, washing his feet, and then kneeling and bowing to the ground like the Mohammedans do. David sat on a Che-chin horse and I took his picture. We finally went on further and found a nice spot to spread our blankets and eat our lunch. After that Bill, Billy, Rassie, and Ed. Midlum started for a hike, the Morrises went in another direction, Reg Smith, Bruce and Pat played ball with David and finally went off for a walk. Agnes, Faith, Lilah and I sat and watched for a long time when Lilah voiced this thought, "Are we really in Russia?" We could have been anywhere.

The hikers got back at five and we started home arriving here about seven o'clock. We sang songs all the way home. David went to sleep. Billy wasn't too tired after six mile hike off into the hills.

Marion Brison's letter home – continued.

November 1, 1939

Dear Folks,

It has been raining hard all day here. I watched the people down on the street for a while going to and from market. I only saw one umbrella. The Russians don't seem to mind the rain.

The lights are so low to-night that we have candles lighted. Most every day they go off entirely about the time we are getting supper and don't come on again until the next day sometime. Dan Volkmar got so upset about lights the other night he took the janitor over to the police station. That didn't do any good of course. He also climbed the telegraph pole to see what he could do. That didn't do any good either.

Nothing matters here. As far as the oil business is concerned they are no farther along than when we came. Nobody cares. Each man should have an interpreter in order to teach the Russian workers but there are only four and they aren't so good.. This is an example. The other day Pat wanted to ask a Russian if they had Nitrogen. The interpreter said he had heard of Walkers gin and Gordons gin but never heard of Nitrogen.

Cars are supposed to be here at 7:30 a.m. for the men. Well, they come anytime between 7:15 and 9:00 and sometimes not at all. They forget to come. Sometimes there are two flat tires in a day which makes a long delay or maybe a mob in the street which can't be broken up to let a car through.

The same night that Dan got all upset about the lights he tried to stop some Russians from taking a goat into the apartment above his. They keep a sheep in the apartment, too. He found out later that this was the most influential family in Grozny that he had stopped on the stairs.

I made a chocolate cake and icing this a.m. and cooked pumpkin and made two pies. Maria went out at noon and came back at five o'clock, stayed until after supper and washed the dishes. She usually comes at 8 p.m. and stays thru until 4 p.m. She is a good soul who has seen better times.

I make all the bread now. It has been good every time. Yesterday I made crackers--never thought I would ever do that. I made crackers in the morning and Billy and David ate them all up right then and there so I made some more in the afternoon. There is a receipe for them in Fanny Farmers cook book.

We have been having pheasant a lot lately. It is very good basted with sour cream as everybody does here. I think about our next experience here will be to buy a pig. Two families will go in together on it--a small one of course. We can fatten it up down in our cellar and then let our Russian women kill it and cut it up. (Bill says we wont fatten it up!) Agnes Midlum and I are going in together. Great life!

Marion Brison's letter home – daily life.

I don't get far with my knitting here because I have to cook too much. Making bread and churning butter etc. take time. Maria does all the cleaning up. She takes up the rugs and washes the floors every other day. When the boys come in she washes their shoes. The mud is all that Dan said in that letter and worse. She does the washing without even a wash board. There aren't such things here.

Billy, David and R. C. Smith dressed in halloween costumes and visited the Americans last night armed with flit gun shooters filled with water. They had a gay time. Did I tell you that Billy and David have a dog? He is a little brown fellow with long floppy ears and four while feet. Billy named him Boots. He is cute but leaky! Bill nicknames him "Puddles". The boys spend lots of time taking him down stairs. R. C. has a doog too--in fact all the Americans have dogs or cats. It gives us something to think about.

Marion Brison's letter home – continued.

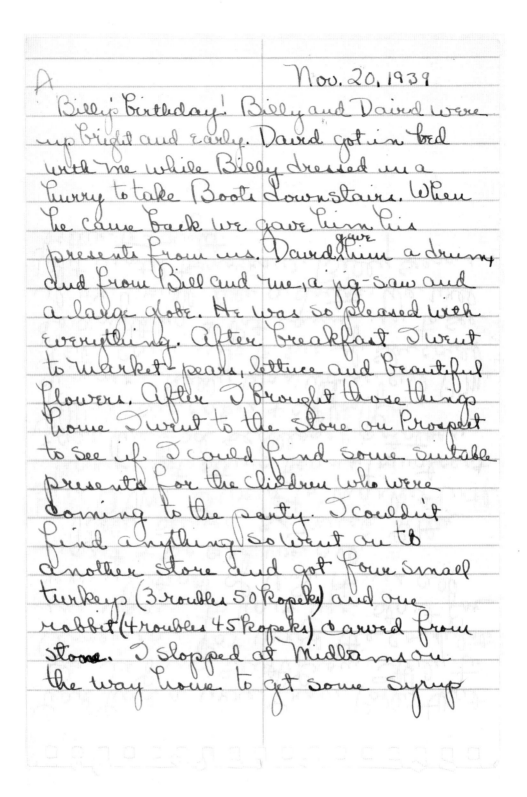

Nov. 20, 1939

Billy's Birthday! Billy and David were up bright and early. David got in bed with me while Billy dressed in a hurry to take Boots downstairs. When he came back we gave him his presents from us. David gave him a drum and from Bill and me, a jig-saw and a large globe. He was so pleased with everything. After breakfast I went to market - pears, lettuce and beautiful flowers. After I brought those things home I went to the store on Prospect to see if I could find some suitable presents for the children who were coming to the party. I couldn't find anything so went on to another store and got four small turkeys (3 roubles 50 kopeks) and one rabbit (4 roubles 45 kopeks) carved from stone. I stopped at Midlams on the way home to get some syrup

Marion Brison's letter home – Billy's birthday.

B

to put in my cake icing.

Billy, Daird and R.C. took their dogs and football over across the river to an open field to play for awhile. Our dinner was a surprise to Billy— his favorite tuna fish with cheese biscuits, fresh pear salad (I wouldn't let them eat the lettuce) string beans and birthday cake.

After that there was a hustle & bustle here. The ice man didn't bring us ice as we expected him to so Mama went to Pat's to get some. Bill was anxious to get the freezer packed for us but had to leave for work. There was the icing to be made, dinner dishes to be done, & the freezer to be turned. Billy helped with that and at 3:30 we were all ready for our guests.

We had place cards, the little turkeys and paper caps on the table and the birthday cake with

Billy's birthday – continued.

ten candles. It looked pretty. Betsy was first to arrive with a Che-chin hat with white fur. Billy was so surprised and happy! He wore the hat most of the afternoon. Mary came with an airplane game, R.C. a wind up machine gun that sparks, Mrs. Greenspon gave him a bar of chocolate which really tastes like American chocolate. Betty Morris brought over an erector set in the morning. Billie Morris, Betsy, R.C., Billy and Daird sat at the table and had ice cream and cake and the rest of us had cake. Billy blew out the candles on his cake. After that the children played games, pinning the tail on the dog (Billie Morris got the prize of a stick of gum) and throwing beans into a bowl. R.C. got that prize getting 6 out of 10 beans

Billy's birthday – continued.

30

into the bowl.

After everybody left Bill and I
had a little lunch (Daivd & Billy
weren't hungry) and I got Daivd to
bed while Bill and Billy worked
on the erector set. Daivd couldn't
get settled, (excitement I suppose)
and finally got up again. Pat
Willis came with a knife! It's
a beauty (leather with a little
gold on it) with a ~~sharp~~ very sharp blade
and a little knife in a little
~~pocket knife in a~~ pocket on the side.
Was Billy happy! Two things - the
hat and the knife that he has been
longing to have. He put them
both on his desk beside his bed
to-night.

Daivd is so sweet & ~~pleased~~
for Billy about all the presents.
The Smiths gave Daivd the little
tools from their jig-saw set and
this morning he spent a long

time pounding nails into a board to hang the tools on. When Billy saw what David had done he said, "That's neat" and did the same with his tools, which pleased Davry very much.

Billy's birthday – continued.

December 20, 1939

Dearest Folks,

There was great excitement among us Americans to-day. We got our Christmas trees! The man who is hired by the Russians tto take care of the Americans came around to-day and told us to meet him out at the park to pick out our trees. The Russians are allowed to clebrate Christmas openly this year for the first time since the new regime. Thir Christmas is January 1st, however. They trim trees as we do. I went out to the park and picked out the tree and carried it home on my shoulder. Billy and David were here making Christmas tree chains. They were all excited, of course, when I brought it in. We have tried to get into the Christmas spirit, and we who have children taklk lots about it and read "The Night Before Christmas" and really have fun-- mostly talking about what Christmas would be like at home. David wrote his letter to Santa Claus asking for a Che-chin hat, an accordian, two drums (one for Baby Allan) and paints and a wooden doll house he saw here. He also said, "Tell Santa I want a tractor-a big one-balshoy tell him" (Balshoy is the Russian word for big.) He talks about the Russian Santa Claus and wanted him to be sure to understand. I have talked up the tractor because one day when I was walking over in the market past some little two by four buildings which go by the name of stores. I happened to see a tractor on the shelf among the combs, beads and other nick knacks. I pointed to it and the man handed it to me but for a long time couldn't find the key to wind it up. We finally found it and when I found it wouls really go my joy was beyond bounds. We have books for the boys which we bought in London, a checker board and checkers for Billy, an accordian for David, a Russian hat for David--one with fur ear-flaps (he has decided he wants that) a box of paints for each, a rope swing for David and Billy's real present is an order for twenty dollars worth of tools (saw, plane, hammer, etc.) When he gets back home. We can't find much for him. He has been working for weeks down in Smith's bathroom an a present for Mr. Smith's have a fine set of tools and a work bench in their bathroom. R. C. has helped Billy with this present and it has given him something to do for a long time.

December 14th is a day to be remembered for us. Billy was sur swinging on his trapeeze--running and catching it, and somehow he missed it and fell--sat down very hard. Just as that happened Billy Morris came in to tell me there was a registered letter atk the P.O. I went over and got that all excited wondering what it could be. It was from the American Embassy in Moscow--a form letter which was sent to every American-telling us to visit the Embassy in person to have our passports validated before Jan. 1st. Nobody wants t that train ride to Moscow, so there has been some excitement and talk. Pat wired the Embassy asking to have a vice-counsul sent here as there are 19 of us, but they wired back that that couldn't be done Our passports were supposed to be good for a year but this rule was made on

Our passports were supposed to be good for a year but this rule was made on account of the war. I suppose I will write to you from Moscow.

Marion Brison's Christmas letter.

33

Moscow, Russia
January 18, 1940

Dear Dor and Allan,

Maybe by the time you receive this you will have already had a cable from us saying that we are leaving. As things look now it won't be more than two months at the most.

We came up here--left Grozny on the 3rd arrived here on the 5th--to have our passports validated, and have been waiting to get a release from Maehino-import. These Russians care little how long we sit around. After we get the release we go back to Grozny to help get the plants started and then we are through. It's all very long and complicated and I will have some stories to tell you that you will scarcely believe.

We have had some wonderful experiences here. We were invited to dinner at Ambassador Steinhardts home. The children were taken upstairs and the Ambasseder himself came up to see that they had a lunch before they went to bed. Such a beautiful home I never dreamed of ever seeing except in the movies. It was built in the Czar's time. A former Ambaseder fitted with twenty complete modern bathroom besides many other improvements. Bill and I sat between the Ambassedeer and his lady--it was a buffet supper and we sat at small tables. Of course the food was so wonderful to us who have had so little American food. We even had sweet potatoes! After eating peas, carrots, and chicken and potatoes over and over again a variety almost finished us. We are thankful for our Grozny farmers however. We are much better off than the people here in Moscow. Here in the hotel where we get the best of everything, during these two weeks we haven't had milk most of the time, no eggs, no coffee some of the time, and very little chicken and no fresh fruit of any kind--not even apples. After we had eaten there was dancing and talking. I got Billy up, dressed him all up and had him come downstairs because he probably will never have another chance like this.

Billy and I were invited to tea there again on the 12th. It was Dulsie Anny Steinhardts party. She is 13 years old and considered Daird and Betsy too young. While we mother's sat in front of the fireplace and talked, drank tea, and played Chinese checkers, Dulsie Ann took the children on a tour through the house. I would have loved to have gone with them. After that they played games upstairs.

Another thing I want to tell you is that in these two weeks we have seen the coldest weather Moscow has seen in years. The Russians call it "black cold" when the thermometer goes below 30°F. It has been to--50°--so cold that our men could hardly stand going out even tho they wrapped their heads in woolen scarfs and wore all the clothes they could. We walked to the Embassy one day at 20° below and the children all cried coming home even tho it is just a short way. They haven't been out since. We will all be glad to get back to Grozny where the weather is so much warmer. We were supposed to leave here today--the bus was to be here at eleven o'clock this A. M. Bill wouldn't let them take our baggage out of our room until he saw the tickets. He is getting wise to these people. Sure enough they thought they would get us to 2nd class instead of having the international coach as the promised (there are seven families of us enough to fill a whole coach) so we came back to our rooms had lunch and are still waiting. It is now 2 P. M. and no word yet. We probably won't go until tomorrow.

I can't wait to see you dear people. How is our little Allan? Is Dad well now? and Mom?

Love to you and Allan and all

Marion--

Marion Brison's letter from Moscow.

34

February 13, 1940

Dear Folks,

Billy and I have just finished two games of Flinch, one of Old Maid and two games of Authors. Davey was in bed and asleep at 7:30. Bill is working the night 12 hour shift and leaves here at 7:30 P. M. We won't see him again until 9 o'clock tomorrow morning, when he will eat breakfast and go to bed. Tomorrow, being his birthday, we are planning a special dinner for tomorrow night. On account of the shift work, we can't have a party and have all the colony as I wanted to do.

The plant is running now and it looks like we might get out of here sometime. The Russians have to be trained and that will be a job.

The pictures of the baby came, and we just can't stop looking at him. I love the big one. He looks so sweet and happy and healthy. The little one is sweet too. I can't wait to get home sometimes. We all talk and talk about it. How we laughed over Dad's letter telling about putting the play pen around the register and Mom having to climb over it. It's cute the way Allan collects the keys. I know. We enjoyed both the letters so much.

Tell Dor and Allan the Christmas cable came on Christmas Day--I think I forgot that in the Moscow letter--and we were so pleased. I keep thinking I will soon be sending one to you saying that we are leaving. It will be for sure around April 15, if not before. We will all be glad to go.

We got back from Moscow on January 21--the train being some 24 hours late. We all had colds and were glad to get back here in our warm apartment. David had quite a bad cold, but he got right over it, and we are all fine now.

Tell Aunt Carrie her nice letter came--how we enjoyed it-- also the cards from George. I want to write a letter to her. It seems like I am busy every minute. The mail is taking a long time to come through. Some letters, two months. We are just getting the Christmas cards now.

The other day the Morrises came back from market with word that there were oranges and grapefruit. We all rushed over. I got ten oranges and one grapefruit, the oranges 3 roubles, and the grapefruit 10 roubles. They were the first we had had since getting off the Russian boat last August-- and so sour, we couldn't eat them without lots of sugar. What a disappointment! In a day or two, I got three more which were nice. There may not be anymore at all.

Marion Brison's letter home – daily life.

35

There hasn't been any sunshine here for weeks. The
streets have been covered with ice and the children have skated
on the sidewalks up until the last few days, when the ice
has changed to mud which one can hardly wade through. Agnes
Midlam and Betsy, David and I took a walk anyway. We had to
get out even though we were just thick with mud when we got
back. Maria meets us at the door, takes our galashes, and
washes them.

I have always meant to tell you but never remembered when
I was writing that we don't have bedbugs and the cockroaches
aren't too bad here in our apartment. The Midlams live over
an eating place and are almost crazy with the cockroaches.

David has been busy all day making valentines. He has
cut out hearts and painted them red, and then pasted them on
big white hearts and then put a little picture in the middle.
Billy has done his school work and then spent the afternoon
with Billie Morris fixing up some funny valentines for R. C.
Yesterday he went to a church service with R. C. and Billie,
in the only church still in use in this part of the country.
Billy Brison reads a lot--reminds me of Dor in the way he comes
in from outside, sits down, and is lost in a book. It really
doesn't make much difference what he reads--encyclopaedia or
funnies. We brought back a lot of funnies from Moscow-American
Embassy. He has a good many boys' books of Jerry Willis, that
Mrs. Willis has given him. She brought Billy "Tom Brown's
School Days," and David "Pinnochio," as presents when she came
back from America.

I am so anxious to hear about the baby's Christmas. I
know it was ᵱᵱᵱᵤᵵ/ᵵ nice and I know he is having the best of
care. I don't worry about him--you may be sure--but I ᵵᵵdo
want want to see him.

                    Love and kisses

                    Marion

Marion Brison's letter home — continued.

Grozny U.S.S.R
Feb. 26, 1940

Dear Aunt Julia,
    Thank you for the cards
I am trading stamps and old
tzar money. I have bought
some stamps and traded some
There's a boy that trades stamps
with us. It is very muddy here
and Billie and me (Tha) take long
walks. One day we went to the
park of Rest and Culture. There was
ice on a pond and Billie walked on
it, and it broke and she went
down knee deep. Other time we
followed the river, and got in
mud ankle deep. When I got
home our maid had to wash
my knickers.
    We have a newspaper. R.C.
is Advertising Manager and
Billy is the Editor and I am
the Distribution Manager. Here
is a paragarph.
    "A Birthday Celbration
    "A dinner party was given last
week in honor of the advertising

Billy Brison's letter home.

manager's 15th birthday. Games were played, presents were given and delectable food was eaten by the the lucky guests. If Mr. R. E. Smith Jr. wishes to find out what was served at the dinner he may apply to this office for the information, as we know he was too busy buttering bread for the tots to pay any attention to the food. With Mademoiselle Betsy M. on his right and

Master David Brison on his left, there he sat with a worried look on his face, no doubt thinking that it was much better to be guest than host." How is everybody.

Your Nephew
Billy B.

Chronology
World War II
Brison Family

1939

March 15th Hitler enters Prague as a conqueror

July 14th "We're off" Brisons leave New York to sail to London then through Kiel Canal

July 25th to August 13th in Leningrad

August 23rd Hitler and Stalin sign Non-Aggression Pact

August 31st Brisons move into "own apartment" in Grozny

September 30th, 1939 "Germany and Russia invade Poland: Britan declares war

October 13th American families advised to leave Gronzy

October 22nd American group goes into the mountains for a picnic

1940

January 2nd 200,000 Soviet troops attack Finland, 57° below zero

January 3rd American group make long trip to Moscow to re-validate passports

January 18th Brisons dine with U.S. Ambassador Steinhardt

February 13th Americans return to Grozney

Russian wounded in Grozny Hospital. *Billy Brison visits*

April 9th Hitler invades Denmark and Norway

Americans leave Grozny for USA via Istanbul, Athens, Brindisi and Naples

April 14th Brisons leave Naples on the Conte di Savoia, the last ocean liner to leave Italy for the US. Arrive in New York City to find Grandma dying in Paterson, N. J., hospital after auto crash on way to meet boat.

May 10th Dutch and Belgians fall to Nazi blitzkrieg

June 4th Allied forces evacuated from Dunkirk

June 14th German troops parade down the Champs Elysees

Book Two
Grozny Revisited
1991

Assisted by the Archbishop of Canterbury, Bill Brison and his wife, Peggy, went back to Grozny. They arrived in the middle of a revolution. The Holy Grail was to find out more about how a remarkable priest was able to keep the Grozny Orthodox Church of St. Michael and All Angels alive when all over the Soviet Union churches were being shut. The following is an abstract of their report to the Archbishop.

Grozny is a city of 400,000 people, the capital of the Chechin Ingush Republic, which is in the North Caucasus (that is, between the Black and the Caspian Seas north of the Caucasian Mts.) The city was established in the mid-19th century as a fort to defend the area against the resident Chechins. Otherwise it is notable mainly for its oil wells and oil refinery, which began to be developed under the czars. My father brought us with him in 1939 and 40 when he was employed by an American oil firm which was helping to install the oil refinery in Grozny. This was a part of my reason for going to Grozny, the other part being that I wanted to explore the history of the Orthodox Church in Grozny. The story that I remember was that the priest had been told by the communists in 1917 that he could keep the church open so long as he was alive. He was an elderly man in 1917, when we were there in 1940 he was ancient and knew that he couldn't live much longer. He was trying to give the Americans icons to make sure that they would be preserved. The communists commonly discarded the icons, burned them or whatever, and dealt harshly with people who kept icons in their houses. I had hoped to do some research on the church under communist rule. This did not prove to be possible for reasons which I will mention later.

We began the trip with a certain amount of uncertainty because almost down to the end we weren't certain that the Russian Orthodox Church was going to provide the kind of hospitality that we needed if we were to make the trip. That is, we needed to know that we wouldn't have to pay tourist hotel rates for the time we were there. They seem to run somewhere between £50 and £100 a night. I had been corresponding with the Moscow Patriarchate for two years but arrangements for our visit hadn't been finalized. Also, we had had no contact with Grozny or the church in Grozny, except through the Moscow Patriarchate and we weren't certain they were expecting us or would provide hospitality. I phoned the Moscow Patriarchate several times and as late as Monday the 2nd of September (the day before we were due to fly) we weren't certain that suitable arrangements had been made for our coming. As it turned out, when we got to Grozny we found out that they had only two days notice of our arrival. But we had paid for our air fare and would have had to forfeit that, so we decided to go anyway, stay in Moscow, if we weren't able to go on to Grozny, for as long as we could afford it and hope we could change our return air tickets and come back. Technically, the ticket was booked for the 30th of September and we shouldn't have been allowed to change it, but Intourist said it probably would be possible. This left a lot of question marks. At any rate, we went; and found that we were met at Moscow Airport (inside the barrier, by the way) by a man named Alexander. It was typical of Alexander that he was able to get inside the barriers somehow, and he was one of the first people to greet anybody who came. There must have been another fifty to a hundred people outside the barrier waiting to greet people. He introduced us to Tamara, who turned out to be his wife, and we went off to find his car. It wasn't too auspicious a beginning as he had to start the car by crossing two wires and the airport was jam packed with cars all honking at each other and very little evidence of any real organisation. Alexander turned out to be quite an interesting person. He had taken a history degree at Moscow University. He had been working at the Lenin Museum in Moscow just off Red Square. He had just lost his job because the museum had been closed as a result of revisionist thinking about Lenin himself. He was in the unusual position in the Soviet Union therefore of being unemployed. His wife, Tamara, worked for the Moscow Patriarchate in the Department of Protocol, and it was she who really provided the contact. Alexander had gone to what they call The White House (the house of the Russian Republic Parliament) when the attempt was made to overthrow Gorbachev to defend Yeltsin and the Parliament from the putsch. (August 19th, 1991) He showed us where the tanks had drawn up and stopped and described how he and others had talked things over with the troops who, in the final analysis, refused to obey orders to move in on the Parliament; so the coup d' etat was defeated.

Alexander took us to our hotel, the Leningradskaya. We had a room on the 16th floor giving a good overlook of that part of the city. On the way to the hotel he drove by several things of interest including the White House, the statue of Karl Marx which had the inscription "proletariat of the world unite" to

Marx Statue.

KGB Founder.

which graffiti had been added to read, "proletariat, we are ashamed". He showed us where the statue of the founder of the KGB had been thrown down and removed and then, the next day, he took us to Red Square where we took photographs of the new Russian flag flying over the Kremlin as well as St. Basil's Church and Lenin's Tomb. We saw on the news that they are even thinking of taking down Lenin's Tomb and burying him next to his widow. But glasnost would not be complete until they got back behind Stalin to Lenin who hijacked the revolution and started the reign of terror that became more associated with Stalin. In Red Square they were collecting for a cathedral which had been on the square and demolished by the communists. They had a painting of the cathedral as it had been and we, at Alexander's suggestion, (although he was not a believer) made a contribution to the cathedral. He took us to our plane (got stopped twice by the police, once for a traffic violation and once a routine check). There had been several telephone calls exchanged and it was finally decided that Grozny was safe for us to visit. They had phoned the local bishop and the bishop had said that there was some unrest in Grozny and that it wasn't safe, so they checked and re-checked and finally decided we could go ahead. We asked several times about payment of the hotel bill and so forth, but that was paid for by our hosts, the Moscow Patriarchate.

Alexander left us at the airport knowing that the plane was delayed. As it turned out it didn't fly until almost 1.00 a.m. There didn't seem to be anybody else going to Grozny. We turned out to be the only foreigners on the plane going to Grozny. They have departure lounges for Russians and lounges for foreigners. We waited in the lounge for about six hours with a very mixed group of Americans, English, Africans, Asians, etc. Finally it was announced in Russian that the plane was due to depart. The sign boards weren't working, there was no announcement in English and if I hadn't heard the word "Grozny" it is possible we might have missed the plane altogether. At any rate, we were shown on the plane and for a long time there were just three of us on board. Then the Russians came aboard and the plane was full. We sat next to a Russian native of Grozny who is living in Germany and spoke German. Her name was Olga. She was very anxious and worried about the situation in Grozny, said "War" and made the sounds "bang, bang, bang", so we weren't in a very good mental state on the flight to Grozny.

We arrived, and were met by a man who didn't speak English and by a policeman. We spent a frustrating few moments but finally established the fact that he had been sent by the church to meet us. His name is Viktor. He took us into the airport security guard's room and we waited until our luggage miraculously appeared. We went out to what turned out to be the church

43

Grozny Barricade across main road to Town Square.

Chechin Demonstration in Town Square.

minibus and Peggy was presented with flowers by Ena, another representative from the church. Igor drove us to our hotel in Grozny. When we got there we found that there was a demonstration in progress (at 4.00 a.m.) with at least hundreds and maybe thousands of Chechen milling about in the square. They had barricaded the square with six or eight large busses and trams so that no vehicle could get in. We had to pass the barricade to get to our hotel, which was

Grozny Communist Party Headquarters (KGB).

adjacent to where the demonstration was going on. When we reached the hotel room, we found that they had arranged a supper for us and so we sat down to a very nice supper with champagne and cognac. A hospitable welcome. It was noisy, but we were very tired (now 4.30 a.m.) and we didn't have any trouble sleeping.

We slept until about noon the next day, (Thursday, 5 September) when we had arranged for Viktor and Ena to come to see us. They brought with them two ladies from the University, Maya and Ludmilla, university professors in the English Dept. As it turned out they were assigned, or rather volunteered themselves and others, to serve in relays to interpret for us. This didn't help us to learn Russian as quickly, but it certainly helped tremendously in our communication. Our visit would have been a lot of signs and gestures and smiles and frustration otherwise. We were to have our meals some distance from the hotel we were staying in, and we were taken there by Igor or Viktor in the church minibus.

We had a rest for a couple of hours and then went to a restaurant with Fr. Piotr and Tanya, a new volunteer interpreter (also a teacher at the University). A band arrived at the restaurant to greet us. They even played two Beatles songs. We had tomatoes, rissoles, meringues and cognac. Some men came by with some bottles of champagne. The band played on, gypsy music and Chechin songs.

At some point on Friday, September 6th, we managed to locate the Dynamo Stadium where my father had played tennis in 1939-40. I was jogging at the time and ran around the Stadium track. This attracted interest, some people in the stands shouting encouragement and others coming up to greet me as I ran. This presented difficulties. I find it difficult to jog and talk at the same time. Some cheered when I managed to sprint across the finish line.

Dynamo Stadium Bill Brison running.

I
The Second Revolution

It has been evident from the time of our arrival in Grozny that this area, in common with the whole of the Soviet Union, was undergoing a second revolution, probably to be as far-reaching as the Bolshevik Revolution of 1917. There was no question that the communists from Lenin on have been thoroughly discredited, and there was little or no support for them or their policies. The Chechins had been demonstrating for two weeks, we were told, although it may have been much longer. They were demonstrating 24 hours a day, 7 days a week, continuous with loud speakers, dancing, soup kitchens set up, people coming in from the surrounding countryside. Grozny is the major city in a republic of the Russian Federation called Chechin Ingush. The Chechins number about 1 million people, the Ingush about 300,000 people, and the Russians somewhere in between, with about 500,000 people. So the Russian people are in a considerable minority in the Republic consisting of only about one quarter of the total. The Republic had a Chechin president elected by the people, but the demonstrations were to get him to resign. It was all happening on our doorstep because the hotel was right next to the area where the demonstrations were taking place. We stayed in the hotel only two nights, but on Friday evening hundreds of Chechins began to stream by the hotel going toward the demonstration – one group numbered at least 100, running and chanting as they went. It was worrying and our interpreter for the time, Maya, was obviously very frightened. She asked us if we would come home with her because she said it would be safer, and she hustled us out of the hotel before Igor could show up with the minibus. We took a minimum of clothing and left everything back at the hotel, along with a note to Igor. As it turned out, we found out they solved the problem of the resignation of the president that evening by dragging him (by the heels) into their headquarters building that they had taken over and forcing him to sign a letter of resignation. Father Piotr was there at the time, and they almost knocked him down when they dragged the president in. Father Piotr is a very large man, about 6ft 2in and probably close to 20 stone. It is interesting that, in a Republic where the majority are not Russian Orthodox Christians, he should be very much involved (as he was) in the political situation. Moscow had sent for him twice to come and consult and to give a reliable report on what is going on here.

Ludmilla, Liza and Piotr.

Chechin General Statue. Tolstoy's Hadji Murat?

The Chechins are Muslim inhabitants of the area. The town of Grozny was established by the Russian General Yermalou about 200 years ago to serve as one of a string of forts which was to keep the Chechins and other non-Russian people in line. Grozny means "fierce". The Chechins have a distinctive style of dress more associated with the Cossacks in western minds, that is, the fur hats and bullets on the vests of their long outer garments. When we were here in 1939-40, we purchased several of their knives. They are about 15 inches long, sometimes decorated with silver and ivory. It was said at that time that a Chechin proved his manhood by killing a Christian. There weren't many Christians around so this meant, in effect, a Russian. My mother wrote that each Chechin had three wives and it was a sight to see them walk through the market with their wives trailing along behind carrying their produce or goods. They were deported by Stalin in 1944. I remember this being reported in the western press and being astounded that one could deport a whole people. They were allowed to return by Krushchev in the mid-1950s. However, they have a long history of feelings of grievance against the Russians and against the communists in particular.

Lenin Pedistal.

They had knocked down the statue of Lenin about a week before we arrived, cut it into pieces and taken it and dropped it in the river. The communist party headquarters, which was directly across the square from the Hotel Kabkas where we first stayed, had been evacuated some time before (we were told two months or two years, we don't know which) but it was empty and it was going to be made into a hospital. The demonstrations didn't end after the Chechins forced the resignation of the president. They were carrying on until they got all officials to resign and until a list of demands was met. These demands had been posted on the former communist party headquarters, but we weren't able to read them and hadn't wanted to stand around long enough to try to decipher them. The Russian people were frightened, there is no question about that. Several of the younger people in particular have said that they will be leaving Grozny because they no longer feel safe. On the night that they forced the resignation of the president there was some gunfire which was described to us as "celebratory shooting". The situation seemed calm in many respects but when you get large numbers of people, and there must be not hundreds but thousands at the demonstrations, then the potential for violence is there. We have been told there were rapes and killings. Russian schoolchildren aren't able to use the tram. There are groups constantly arriving from the countryside, numbering from 50 to 100 joining the main mass of the demonstrators, sometimes small groups marching off following a green flag, which is the Chechin/Muslim emblem. On the other hand, away from the square life seems to go on as usual and there is not any sign of breakdown of public order. In the last few days they began removing the barricades from the square, that is they had taken three or four of the buses which blocked the square off away, but they have not really opened up the square for other vehicles. The green flag now flies, or was flying, over the former communist party headquarters. The local situation has been the lead story on Moscow television, so it is considered serious. It is difficult on the ground to know how things are going. Father Piotr is right in the middle of it and would be a good source of information but, although we have spent some time with him, the occasions were not such that I wanted to mention the political situation. Also, I imagine his usefulness depends upon his discretion, and I wouldn't think he would want to say too much to westerners at this time. It may be that we'll get a chance to talk to him about the situation confidentially at some point, and I am sure he can shed more light upon it than anybody else. It is interesting that an orthodox priest in this area should be in this situation. When I referred to his activity and said that it was good that he was able to help reconcile the situation; he replied through his interpreter that "the job of a priest is to bring peace". He is an impressive man but obviously suffering physically and emotionally. He has a bit of a twitch which several people have noticed and which doesn't seem to be natural with him. This is not the best time in the world for us to be dropped on him. On the other hand, he seems to have enough assistance so that we can be taken care of by other people.

We talked to Aslan, the one male professor at the university who is also a Chechin and also a Muslim. Aslan said that 95% of the Chechin population

Bulldozer clearing mountain road. Driver surveying rocks from top.

died when the Chechins were subdued by the Russians in the middle of the 19th century. That the percentage was this high was disputed by other Russians we spoke to. He also said that about 50% of the Chechins died (frozen or starved to death) in the deportation in 1944. No one contested this and it seemed a reasonable figure under the circumstances. We talked to several Chechins about their own personal history and they were consistent with each other. For instance, the bulldozer driver who was clearing a mountain road deep in the Caucasian Mts. had the following story. He was a little boy in 1944. His mother left him and his two little brothers to go down to the market to buy them clothes (they were naked). She was seized, along with other Chechins, by Soviet troops for deportation. She was not allowed to go back to get her sons but was allowed to send clothing to them. They were also taken and deported. They didn't see their mother for another four years. The irony of the situation is that their father had died at Stalingrad fighting with the Red Army in defence of his country and family. The bulldozer operator was a most courageous (or foolish) man. I saw him operating his bulldozer and, from my Marine Corps experience, know the danger that he incurred. He was clearing a mountain pass with dynamite and pushing boulders around with his dozer blade. He said that he had the Order of Lenin for his service to his country. We learned from others that the deportation happened in mid-February and that they were sent to Kazakhstan to an area which was a waste land and had not been inhabited before. It took 22 days on the train to get there with no heat and very little food. The communists went through the population and took every Chechin living in Grozny or the Chechin Ingush Republic, no matter what his service had been to this country or what his influence was.

The head of the Supreme Soviet of the Chechin Ingush Republic is a man called Zavgeau Dokku. He is a Chechin, married to a Russian woman, and he was the one who was dragged in by the heels when Fr. Piotr was present, where he was forced to sign a resignation. We heard he later said that he hadn't resigned, at least that his resignation had been extracted by force. He had been constitutionally elected and therefore should not be forced to resign. Also, in the last few days a mob went to the home of the head of the town council, a man named Kutsenko Vitaly. They were, I believe, trying to obtain his resignation. He jumped off his balcony to escape and later died in the hospital as a result of his injuries. As I reported, the demonstrations have been going on continuously and there are two people on hunger strike until their demands are met. The situation may have been resolved this afternoon, that is the 18th of September. A deputy of Boris Yeltsin, a man named Ruslah Khaseulatov, came down from Moscow to help resolve the situation. We are told that he said that the Chechins' demands are reasonable, but that this is not the time to realise them. What they have agreed, apparently, is that the Parliament should be suspended and a Council made up to run the affairs of state. Fr. Piotr was on the Supreme Soviet for this republic and, because he is held in high regard, may very well be on this new Council. The Chechin demands, seem to be mainly: first of all, for the resignation of the head of the Supreme Soviet (the man who was forced to resign and later we heard has resigned) and the Supreme Soviet en masse as well as the head of the Town Council, who died in the hospital. So that's the first set of demands – the resignation of the officials, or at least some of the officials, in Soviet government. The second demand is for independence. Most of the Russians feel that this is ridiculous because Chechin-Ingush is simply not able to exist as an independent entity. They are land-locked, surrounded by other republics of the Russian Federation, except for Georgia to the south, which is seeking independence itself but the Caucasian Mountains lie between.

The Chechins took away the barricades around what I've been calling the square, which I guess is still accurate – it's a road through the centre of Grozny. It caused annoying blockage of traffic when it was barricaded off; but they took away all the busses, trams and the steel sewer pipes and the rubble, so the whole area is open for traffic. That happened on the 20th of September. This presumably was because their demands had been met. I don't believe I've said yet how the demands were met. The Supreme Soviet resigned and was replaced by a Provisional Committee whose responsibility is to map out future legislation which will allow for an elected assembly. This followed the resignation of the former Supreme Soviet of this Republic. This Provisional Committee is composed of members selected from various interest groups within Grozny and the province generally. These consist of Chechin, Ingush, Russian, also of smaller ethnic groups apparently, also of religious groups like the Muslims, the Christians (Orthodox) and the Jewish people. How were these people selected? The Chechins continued to demonstrate after this, because they felt that some of the people selected for this Provisional Committee were simply former members of the Supreme Soviet who weren't acceptable to them because they supported the old regime. They ceased to demonstrate, apparently, when their further demands had been met. Even so, the hunger strikers appear to be still in the tent (although I'm not sure of that) in the square opposite the governmental capital building next to the Hotel Kabkas. When we passed by on Sunday there was a much smaller demonstration by the Chechins being addressed by a man with a loud speaker in front of that governmental building where the large demonstrations had been taking place.

Other information. Tanya told us that her sister works at the television station and the station had been taken over by an armed force who was stationed there and forcing the people to continue to work, but of course getting out their own propaganda line. Her sister was frightened, she said; on the other hand the Chechins and Muslims, generally speaking, have an obligation to behave in an honourable fashion. Another little insight. We had a conversation with Viktor last evening, and I asked him if he thought it was actually dangerous for us if I had gone out and taken photos during the height of the demonstration. He said he thought not, because the Chechins thought of themselves as in the right and "big men" and were quite happy to have anyone come and publicise what they were doing. This was corroborated by Aslan, so I think that, in retrospect, our leaving the hotel was probably not necessary; and I think Maya panicked. However, the other side of it is that when you get thousands of people demonstrating and some of those people at least had supported Saddam Hussein in Iraq, that it was quite possible that they might also have made the association between us (that is, Anglo-Americans) and the whole mess that they were in. It probably was just as well to get out at that time. My, only regret is that we didn't follow Viktor's advice rather than Maya's, whatever that would have been, but that's problematical. We relied on the people we thought we could rely on at the time.

On Thursday, 18th September, the demonstrations ended and the situation seems to be much calmer. The Russian people don't seem to be as worried as they were. We went to Church on Sunday morning to attend a wedding, visited the Sunday School. The children recited prayers and poems for us; we went to a Baptism. We met with Ludmilla, Fr. Piotr's wife, their daughter is in Sunday School and was in one of the schools we visited. I commented that although the democratically elected government had been undemocratically removed from power, the good thing was that violence had been avoided except in a couple of cases like the mayor and the chairman of the council. Ludmilla replied that they came very close to the brink of violence, and I think that certainly was true. The other fact that I have forgotten to report is that Aslan said that one of the first things that the Chechins did when they began to be active after the putsch was defeated was to go into the KGB building and turn them out. He said there was no need particularly to worry about our visas only allowing us to visit in the Grozny area because there was nobody around to check on us. I'm not sure that is exactly true because there are local police forces and they would perhaps check.

We talked to Imran, who took us to the mountains with Helen (24th September). We asked him about the revolution and he said that the

St. Michael's Wedding – four couples.

demonstrations had lasted 28 days, and since we know when it ended then we know when it started. He also said that the old Supreme Soviet, the ones who resigned, were dominated by the communists, and there was the suspicion that many of them had supported the putsch. So that's what gave the impetus from central government as well as local Chechins to oust them. I have no reason to believe that that is not true. He also replied that, when I asked my usual question about who selected the new Provisional Committee, they had been selected by the folk. I take it he means the people, but Helen said she had her suspicions about how the selection process went on since, of course, there was no election and who knows how they were selected. Also the demonstrations went on after the selection was made because they didn't like some of the people who had been selected because they were from the old Supreme Soviet. Imran gave us the date of the election, and I think it's the 23rd of November.

II

The Russian Orthodox Church in the Chechin Ingush Republic

We met Fr. Piotr, and on our first meeting he took me behind the iconostasis in the altar area, after first asking if we ordained women. I wonder what the result would have been if I could have "yes" or if I had given my personal opinion. Women are not allowed to go there and so Peggy stayed in the main body of the church. The church itself is well decorated with icons with what I would call a lectern, in the front of it from which the priest preaches his sermons, reads the gospel and which has two icons (one to the Virgin and one depicting Christ). He showed me with great reverence the chalice that they have and the crowns which they use for weddings. Fr. Piotr was very welcoming. We went into his study and were introduced to his wife, his son, Fr. Sergei (his name is pronounced differently from that of a lay man because he is a priest). Sergei's wife, Galina, was also there. We talked a bit about the church and asked questions back and forth. I made a point of saying that we would like to investigate the history of the church and that we would like to talk to some people, both old and young, or groups perhaps, about the church. Fr. Piotr said that he had only been in this parish for five years and so wasn't present in 1939-40, and this seemed to conclude the conversation so far as investigating the history of the church was concerned. I did also say that we would like to talk to some of the clergy, either himself if he were not too busy, or some of his assistant clergy about the liturgy, etc. None of these requests have been followed up. They have been most welcoming and hospitable in every other way, but we haven't been able to engage in the kind of conversations with people which I would have liked. I think I may know some of the reasons for this. We had a visit today (18th) from Ella (Eleanor) and she explained a few things to us. Eleanor is an interesting contact because she is both a student at the university studying English and a very active and faithful member of the church. She served as a liaison with Fr. Piotr. and Fr. Sergei and their wives; she was the catalyst for several very fruitful discussions about the Orthodox Church and she seemed to know the practice vis a vis theory. She invited us for a meal at her home and told us her mother would be the one to know about the 1917 priest.

This didn't seem to be the case. Maya came with us to Church and this provided another perspective because she was a convinced atheist. It was her daughter, Lena, who was baptised while we were there. We saw her at the first meeting we had with the students at the university and then the next Sunday I spotted her in the congregation when we went to the liturgy. She also attends Fr. Piotr's Sunday afternoon Sunday School which seems to go on for three or four hours. She has asked me several questions, more or less on the run, about spirituality (the last being why Christ died for us on the cross!) She is married with a two year old son and her husband would like her to go to his home area, which is near the Urals.

She is one of those people who seems to grasp the problem and has spoken to us frankly about the situation in the Orthodox Church. That situation is that the church is still very traditional, to a degree that I had not even thought of, much less underestimated. We had observed that the Liturgy is in Old Slavonic, which Fr. Sergei told us was understood by people who come to church regularly – we're not so sure. Ella said she understood some of the prayers because she had sung in the choir and could see the text but she, after all, is a very intelligent young woman, a student of linguistics, and a very diligent worshipper. Another way of expressing this was that when Ella talked about how she could come closer to God and the fact that Fr. Piotr's Sunday School doesn't entirely meet her requirements, I suggested the possibility of gathering together a small group and studying the Bible. She said that this was illegal, as far as the church is concerned. The idea is, apparently, that only the clergy are seen as fit to convey the meaning of scripture to the people. She also explained in the course of our conversation that Old Slavonic was the language of the people in Russia before the revolution and that modern Russian, which incorporates many western and other non-Russian words, came about only after the 1917 Revolution. The idea is, and she at least partly agrees with this, that Old Slavonic is more beautiful and preserves the purity of language and expression. In his Bible study, she said, Fr. Piotr reads the text in modern Russian, comments on it, often adding bits and pieces from his own experience (which she finds helpful) and then reads it in Old Slavonic; but the basic idea of the instruction apparently is that they should learn the language of the liturgy, that is Old Slavonic. The lessons are read in Old Slavonic and the sermons are preached, I take it, mainly in Old Slavonic.

Ella's information corroborates the kind of conversation we had over dinner when Fr. Piotr invited us out to the restaurant and he and Fr. Sergei and wives and their granddaughter Liza, Peggy and I and Viktor and Igor sat around and talked for a while. Fr. Sergei argued with his own father, Fr. Peter, about aspects of worship, but they were generally external details, e.g. as to whether women should or should not wear a hair covering in church. We get the idea that they are not particularly eager to discuss the details of their liturgy even on the basis of my asking questions about symbolism in the services. I did have a very interesting conversation with Fr. Sergei as we were going out to visit the several different village parishes in the area. He was quite open to my questions about the baptism service that we had just seen. He said, among other things, that those being baptised received some instruction before they are baptised. They receive communion up until the age of 5, 6, 7; then they, like everyone else, must confess their sins before they are allowed to receive communion. We noticed that in a congregation of several hundred, only maybe 20 would receive

Congregation in Church (Communion to a baby.)

communion and most of them old ladies or children under 7 or so. I presume this is because they others haven't confessed their sins. It is always difficult through interpreters to make sure that you are getting the right point across in the right way, but we have asked several times in several different ways and have expressed the desire to sit down and talk to the clergy about the liturgy and with lay people about the church, and there has been no response; whereas there has been a very quick response to almost everything else that we have suggested, so I think there is a real reluctance among them to do this, and we will just have to accept it. It seems to me that the Russian church is caught somewhere between the Latin Mass and Cranmer and that many of the things that happened in the western church at the time of the reformation and which we in the Church of England accept for granted, e.g. reading of the scripture by the people and their ability to interpret it in situations such as bible study groups, are not accepted at all in the Russian Orthodox Church. We have been told this by Ella.

Upon reflection, I don't believe I (and probably most westerners) really understood the effect of Russia's isolation from the rest of Europe. There are many reasons for this: its history in repelling and absorbing Tartar invasions from the East and therefore having a different culture from the rest of Europe, its sheer size, its backwardness relative to other European countries, and the despotism of the czars. Since the Russian Revolution in 1917, the Iron Curtain has isolated Russians for another 70 years from developments in the western world. They haven't been allowed to travel outside the country (or even within their own country) without official permission, which was hard to get. They haven't had the kind of interchanges in business, culture, education, etc. to a degree which would have opened up the country to outside influences. Thus, in many ways, I think they are the other side of the Protestant Reformation in Europe. They certainly don't see it this way and believe that theirs is the one true way, although their absolute certainty on this point makes it difficult for them to enter into free discussion.

Baptism

We have been to two baptismal services. These are done in a separate area not even a part of the church building but a baptistery which is obviously set aside for that purpose although it is also used for Fr. Piotr's Sunday School. Those being baptised, and they come in a variety of ages from babies on up to middle aged adults, arrange themselves around the sides of the room with their godparent behind them. The babies are naked, men and boys are stripped to the waist and women wear a brief gown which usually leaves their back exposed. The service is about an hour long. Once again, it is done in Old Slavonic. When I asked Fr. Sergei if the people make any baptismal promises, he said they used the Creed but because most of the people couldn't recite the Creed it was said for them by the priest. I might add here that Maya's daughter, Lena, decided to be baptised while we were here and she asked me to be her godfather, so we know a bit more about baptism through her experience than we would otherwise. When she went before, I take it several months at least and perhaps a year ago, she was refused baptism but not, I take it, after any extensive interview or consideration of her reasons for wanting to be baptised. She didn't receive any instruction to speak of about baptism before she went and she was rather

St. Michael's Baptisms – adults and infants.

ignorant of the details, as were the other people who were there. By details I mean such things as the fact that you have to wear a certain kind of gown because they do splash a lot of water around during the baptism and that women are not allowed to wear make-up. One of the mothers who came in had quite a bit of make-up on and she got a severe ticking off from the priest (not Fr. Piotr or Fr. Sergei).

Lena's baptism. We went into the room and the priest, who is very friendly, showed me where to stand. Lena stood in front of me. There were about 18 people being baptised that day, and this was one of two baptisms on Saturday. I can really describe only what happened and not what was said, since I didn't understand and Lena didn't understand the words of the liturgy either. Once again, she is an intelligent young woman and speaks a fair amount of English, but she couldn't understand the prayers of the liturgy. The baptism, then, consisted of a good deal of chanting by the priest and there was one of the everpresent lay women there, an older woman, who sang the responses. During the course of the service, there were two anointings with oil where the priest takes a brush He anoints first the forehead with the sign of the cross, then the ears, then the cheeks, then the mouth, then the breast, then the back of each hand, and then the top of each foot.

When we came to the baptism itself, the candidates go forward, the priest takes the naked baby and dips him in the font, holds him down there and splashes water on him. When it is a child or an adult tall enough they stand, they bend over and put their hands down in the font with their head into it also, (it's quite a large vessel), and the priest sprinkles water on them three times and liberal amounts of water on their head, the back of their neck and their back, so quite a bit of water splashes on the floor also. Two of the women were not very well prepared, or probably hadn't been told, what was expected. Lena only knew because she had come to the baptism before with us. These two young women both had their sweaters on and so they got quite wet, and I take it that's not the way it should be done. They really should have some kind of a special baptismal gown on so the priest can do the job properly, so to speak. In addition to the water and two anointings with oil, they go around and the woman who is assisting the priest gave each candidate and each godparent a lighted candle. Then we were all told to turn right and we walked around the room twice while the priest chanted. There was also another interesting bit of symbolism when the priest looked toward the congregation so that we could see him (some of the time he was pointed toward an icon in what would be the east wall) and he blew three times, once to the left, once up and down, and once to the right – making the sign of the cross while expelling air through his lips. I assumed this has something to do with the Holy Spirit – I found out later that he is blowing the devil out. Also, during the service the priest brought the cross around to be kissed, and he made a special point of coming to me first to present the cross, which I duly kissed, and then he went on to the other godparents and candidates. Following the service, Lena invited us to her home for a meal. It was interesting that during that meal I had a chance to ask her gently what kind of instruction she had and what she knew about baptism. It turned out she knew very little and so we spent about an hour or so talking about the meaning of baptism, incorporation into the body of Christ, using mainly St. Paul's symbolism. There was a lot more that could have been said. The priest had told her to receive communion at 7.30 the next morning (Sunday) and so we went to the liturgy at that time together.

The workload on the priests was enormous. The church was growing enormously, with Muslin converts. Fr. Piotr delegated as much of the teaching load as possible, but he and Fr. Sergei were expected, by custom or decree to do most of it. Even the other assistant priests apparently weren't qualified to teach.

The Divine Liturgy

We walked to Church through streets crowded with Russians and Chechins. I wore my black cassock and clerical collar as a means of identification and of making the point that I was an official visitor from a brother church. Anglicans and Orthodox have always been close because we have similar positions on important matters, especially vis-a-vis the Roman Catholic Church. If I had thought of it I would have contacted the Anglican Orthodox Fellowship before we left England. I soon stopped wearing the cassock because of the hostility of Chechins on the street. And I noticed the Orthodox priests wrapped up closely when they left the Church premises. There was no point in courting trouble, but I continued to wear my clerical collar.

The liturgy the next morning began at 6.30. We were told to come at 7.30. This is fairly standard practise even among the devout because the services go on for so long. I'll describe the service briefly. The church is decorated with icons along all the walls and particularly on the iconostasis which separates the altar from the people. The first icon on the right of the centre door represents Christ, the first on the left is the Madonna, the second on the right represents the Patron Saint. As a special honour we were shown into kind of a balcony arrangement which we had to ourselves as we had on the previous Sunday when we had gone to church. I wasn't too happy about this because it separated us from the people, but it did make it possible for Peggy to sit down and to observe a little more readily what was going on. The people spend a lot of time crossing themselves – they do it in the Orthodox fashion, of course, and at the conclusion of crossing themselves they bow low. There are times when most people seem to be doing this, but there is no great uniformity about the time at which they do it. There is someone in church at almost any given moment who is crossing himself or herself. The congregation is made up mainly of old ladies but with a sprinkling of men and younger people. There is a constant coming and going which doesn't disturb the liturgy really because it is all done in a sensible fashion. People also buy candles, and if they are not close enough to the candle holder, they pass them forward to the places where the candles are lit; and often there was a person stationed there whose main function seemed to be to light the candles as they come up and to take out the exhausted candles if there are more than can be lit – I think they were just storing them on the candle holder and lighting them at a later time. This seems to be very important to them. The service is quite lengthy and ended somewhere around 9.30. Everyone is standing up all the time except for those few of us sitting in the balcony. At one point two ladies came out with trays receiving the collection and just wove their way through the congregation. There were approximately

300 people there. It was fairly closely packed and so it took them quite some time while the liturgy was going on, and people would simply put money on their trays. I went downstairs and stood in the body of the church so I could make an offering. Also, I wanted to be there for the communion and was a little uneasy about being in the balcony for too long. After a while Lena came down and went forward and she received Holy Communion as those newly baptised had been told to do and then she came and stood by me for the rest of the service. The priest starts the service on the congregation side of the iconostasis, then he goes in and there are several comings and goings when the doors of the iconostasis are either open so the people can see the communion table or closed. He comes out at one point with something (it was hard to tell what it was) for reverence and goes back in, then he comes out with the chalice and with communion. Communion is administered with a spoon – I believe there is bread dipped in the wine and he puts it in each person's mouth. I didn't go forward for communion while I was in Grozny since, as I remembered it, the Russian Orthodox Church did not permit this. I didn't have any opportunity to ask Fr. Piotr until Monday the 23rd September after the last service in Grozny which we could attend. He answered that you had to go to confession before communion and this was an absolute bar. I didn't press on this point because I felt that it was said in such a way as to indicate that he didn't think it was possible in any case. I also had grave reservations about the hygiene of the operation since everyone uses the same spoon and it's all dipped into the same chalice. I'm not overly scrupulous about these matters, but that does seem to me a bit much. In any case, the great majority of people in the church don't receive communion. It seems to be mainly children, even of an age who have to be held by their parents or grandparents, (one baby who looked no more than one month old) and the newly baptised like Lena. I wouldn't say there were more than 20 people who received communion in a congregation that exceeded 300. I would like a further explanation of what is happening in the liturgy, and perhaps I'll get a chance to ask Fr. Sergei, who seems to be the most forthcoming; and so I'll include that if I have that opportunity.

Some general impressions of Orthodox worship.

The church is located behind a high fence with a high metal gate which it is impossible to see over – it must be about 10 feet high – through which cars can come (it is always closed) with a smaller gate for pedestrians. The latter is usually closed but on Sundays it's open with a few beggars clustering around the entrance, old ladies and a young woman with a child on one occasion. As you come into the church courtyard, there is a series of booths with roofs (kind of

Maingate St. Michael's Church.

like an open shed arrangement) ranged along the fence of a fairly narrow courtyard. These booths we found also in Fr. Antony's, and we learned from him that these booths are to shelter people during rainy or cold weather; and they also serve as a place for people to sit out of the sun. In the courtyard there are booths connected with the church where they sell candles and some cakes that people seemed to be eating during the service. These are not the bread that is handed out at the end of the service as in the Greek Orthodox Church. But they also do give bread out. We weren't conscious of it because they were doing it after the service is over because they don't have time at St. Michael's here in Grozny to do this at the end of the service; but it is their custom also to give out this bread to each worshipper. We always arrived after the service had begun – most people do this because the service goes on for so long, it could begin at 6.30 and be over at 9.30. After Lena's baptism, the morning service on Sunday began at 6.30 but we were told to come at 7.30, so we take it that this is an acceptable time to arrive. People seemed to be coming and going at all times, but most people are present at the time of the apparent consecration and at the time that people receive communion, although relatively few do receive communion. On one occasion in a church that must have had several hundred people coming and going, but at least 300 people at any given time, there were something like 21 children (usually babies brought up for communion and sometimes very young babies) and 34 adults who received communion. The mothers didn't usually receive, but I did notice one mother receiving. There was one man and most of the women were older, all babushka types, with one being pregnant. It occurs to me with their stipulation and absolute ban on receiving communion unless you confessed your sins (and I believe to the priest) beforehand; it might be that only the old ladies who can mumble a word or two can reasonably confess their sins. Some of the younger ones probably don't want to. Children up until 6 or 7 can come to communion without the necessity of confession ahead of time. I always remember Edward Downing saying that most people's idea of sin is connected with sex; and most people who receive communion in the Orthodox Church are those who would have little inclination in that direction. In fact, one of the younger women was very pregnant, so this might not have been a problem in her case either. People are coming and going all the time and everyone stands. They say that sometimes the church is so packed that you cannot even make the sign of the cross because you are too close to people. They stand there, and there are people going forward at different times to light candles, presumably prayers for various people or situations. There are several stations around the church – two up by the altar and others in front of icons – where people also light candles. If the church is too densely packed to make it reasonable for people to get forward, then they just pass the candles forward from worshipper to worshipper until they get to the stand where they are lit. People cross themselves incessantly during the service but not uniformly; there seems to be no time, even at what seems to be the final blessing when the priest comes out with the cross and blesses the people, that everyone signs himself. They do it very meticulously – no scratching your nose along the way, as I remember Dr. Hardy did once – because they believe that they are etching the form of the Christ on the cross on their bodies as they make the sign of the cross. I would suspect that some people sign themselves maybe 50 to 75 times during a normal service. Others don't do it at all. As they sign themselves with the cross they end up with a bow toward the iconostasis, and this is often a very deep bow – sometimes people even touch the floor and sometimes they prostrate themselves, getting down on one knee and touching the forehead (one or two might do this out of 300). There is an air of formality about the service and yet an air of informality. Certainly they are very serious and pay attention to what they are doing while they are doing it, but other things happen that would be amusing to a Church of England congregation. for instance, Matushka Ludmila, Fr. Piotr's wife, has her own little Sunday School group. She brings the older ones into church and they are up to the right of the iconostatis tucked away in a corner but quite prominent.

They appeared to be having a cup of tea during the liturgy. A woman came to Peggy last Sunday and offered her a gift of 3 tomatoes and 9 eggs. She gave her this rather large bag right in the middle of the service. We couldn't understand her and she couldn't understand us, but the intent was obvious, and we thanked her for it. A man came up with a baby in his arms during the service. I was right in the middle of the congregation, and he said he wanted to have his baby baptised – mistaking me, I guess, for an Orthodox Priest. I was happy to have Lena standing next to me and she told me what he had asked; she directed him to the lady who takes care of that kind of inquiry. The way they take up the collection is interesting, it isn't done at a time when it is the principal thing happening. Seemingly at no particular time, although I'm sure there is a time, two old ladies come out with rather large trays and one follows the other through the congregation. They weave their way through, which can be rather difficult if there are a great many people there, and people put their money on the tray as they pass. They usually say a brief thank you each time anyone drops anything in, but if you drop more than ordinary they stop and give you a special thanks. Then the time comes to receive communion, people go forward, not in any kind of order as is done in England, but they just crowd around the priest. The priest administers the sacrament by dipping a spoon into a chalice with the bread and the wine soaking in the chalice. He puts the spoon in the person's mouth with the consecrated bread and wine on it. The deacon is there with a large napkin which extends from underneath the chalice to the person's chin so that they don't spill any on the way, and then the deacon wipes the person's lips after they have received with this same napkin (same area of the napkin for the 40 or so communicants so far as I could see). The babies receive first, young children, and then the babushkas. It all seems to operate quite well and shows that some of our more elaborate and formal arrangements to make sure that people get to the communion rail are not really all that necessary. After receiving communion, most people cross their arms across their chests, their fingertips in the area of their collar bones to make the form of a St. Andrew's cross on their breast. Then they walk from the place where they receive communion, sometimes turning toward the iconostasis and signing themselves and then actually leave the church building. The rest of the people stay there and at a later point in the liturgy the priest comes out. He reads something from a book, which I thought might be the Last Gospel, but Ella, who is quite knowledgeable about worship, wasn't sure what it was because it was in old Slavonic. She didn't think it was a passage from the gospel. Then about the last thing that happens is that the priest comes out with the metal cross and holds it up and people come up and kiss the cross. Since I wasn't invited to, and was pretty sure that I wasn't able to, receive communion, I went forward each time and kissed the cross. Some people also kissed the priest's hand; I didn't do that. They seemed to be very pleased, that is the priest who was celebrating communion for that particular Sunday, seemed to be very pleased that I did that. Generally speaking they seemed to be very pleased that we were there and participating in their worship. Of course, since most people don't receive communion anyway at any given liturgy, then the fact that we didn't was not particularly obvious. We were asked when we were going to be preaching by several people, and I didn't believe that this would be possible either. I thought, as a matter of fact, that there might be some special occasion like during Fr. Piotr's Sunday School class, when I would have been given a few moments to say something to the group, but this didn't happen. I think the reason is that the church is, to an amazing degree, controlled by the clergy and the clergy are controlled by tradition. If I get this straight (and I'm pretty sure that I have from Ella) then the priests don't teach anything but what can be derived from the bible itself and I suspect commentaries on the bible and the writings of the fathers. These, I believe she said, are relatively few in number. Not only this, but I also suspect from what Fr. Antony said (I asked him which seminary he had been to and he said he hadn't had time for that but was hoping to do so fairly soon) that some of the priests are not necessarily very knowledgeable. Some seemed to be there mainly to celebrate and chant the liturgy. When I talked to Fr. Sergei about preparation, it seemed as though the preparation was made before ordination, but on the other hand, Sasha's friend (Misha) is going to be ordained on November 21st at St. Michael's and he hadn't been away to any kind of seminary or theological college apparently. I suspect that some of the priests don't really have much formal theological education. If this is true, then that accounts for the fact that Fr. Piotr didn't seem to want us to talk to them about matters theological. But again with a heart condition with a growing church, at the centre of explosive political situation, a revolution, he didn't have time for theological speculation. He made time to offer his hospitality. The pressure on him while we were there was tremendous.

The music is interesting. The choir sings almost all the service, when there is a choir. When there isn't a choir, there were a group of babushkas in the front left (near as they can get to the iconostasis) who sing or lead the singing – in most cases doing it themselves. The choir is very good. It combines the deep Russian male voice (and there seems to be a tradition of singing deeper than the average male voice would normally – I think some of the priests almost cultivate this.)

It was noticeable that one of the priests has naturally a much higher voice and he was much less impressive. The choir combines the deep male voice with a rather higher than normal female singing; it is a very beautiful combination. The congregation don't sing very much except at one part of the liturgy there is a rather tuneful part (the Lord's Prayer we found out later). The congregation came alive in the singing and I asked (later) what was happening.

One of the interesting features about St. Michael's and the other churches we saw is the number of apparently volunteer and willing helpers around the church. As you come into the courtyard there seem to be usually at any time when there is a regular service, or before that or after it, some 10 or 15 babushkas are around to help. Generally speaking they are doing what needs to be done to keep the church clean and the courtyard tidy, selling candles or helping out in the administration of the parish. There is a lady who sits at a desk on the ground floor of the priest's house and takes care of things like baptismal enquiries. There is the lady I mentioned who was present at the baptism and led the responses (in fact, sung the responses because the congregation didn't know any of them). She also mopped up the floor after the baptism (they spill quite a bit of water they way they do it) and also cleaned up after a baby suddenly urinated during the service – much to the surprise of the godmother who was holding her. I have mentioned the little choir of people who sing the responses when there is no organised choir in the choir loft. There are also a couple of babushkas who cooked our lunch after one of the Sunday services. The babushkas are present to open the gate for motor vehicles and, typically, when we were coming into the compound, Viktor would honk the horn and some little old lady would come running out to open the gate.

When Fr. Piotr saw us out on our last visit as we were walking, and we came to the pedestrian entrance, which was closed, he unlocked it. His granddaughter (Liza) was going to open it when he stopped her and waited until a little old lady came up and opened the door and let us out. Apparently that is her job and she does it. There is this kind of tradition of service – the priests expect to be waited on. Actually, I opened the gates for Igor one day and I can see that this really was a breach of etiquette on my part. It was also interesting to see that when Liza first greeted Fr. Piotr yesterday morning, she went up to him and she kissed his hand and the pectoral cross that he wears and then he made the sign of the cross over her and then she gave him a big hug. Apparently that's the way you greet a priest. I saw a lay person kiss the priest's hand and then touch her forehead to his hand, I believe it was a form of dismissal. I was told that priests greet priests by exchanging a kiss on the cheek, one at normal times but three at Easter, and then they kiss each other's hands. I did this with Fr. Antony, but I forgot about it so far as Fr. Piotr was concerned so I shook hands with him in the western fashion.

III

The University

The university has about 5000 students. It has 40 teachers in the language department alone. They have been very good about supplying a relay of interpreters, professors and some students, at practically any hour of the dry or night to help us out. This meant that we were able to communicate with a wide range of people over a wide range of subjects. The only problem has been really that sometimes there has been a lack of kind of theological background. I was trying to talk with Fr. Piotr, for instance, about basic theological and liturgical matters, and the interpreters didn't have the religious vocabulary. In a way that's been interesting but in a way it's also been a bit frustrating and I didn't think I was really getting to the root of the matter at times or they to what I was trying to say. We were helped in this because a couple of the students are regular church goers or active Christians and we have used them to interpret in the theological discussions later on. The other minor problem has been that this has set back our learning Russian ourselves because there hasn't been much motivation; but that is really not a great problem because we wouldn't have been able to learn enough in a month to make it possible for any real communication except on basics.

The university asked both Peggy and me to lecture, three lectures each. I lectured on contemporary British politics and the western church; Peggy lectured on daily life in Britain and education in Britain. Our lectures were received very well. They are hungry for information about the west. It is a somewhat eerie situation to be talking to a group of 40 or 50 students and professors who speak English quite well with an English accent, have a very good knowledge and are well read in English literature, but who have never talked to a native English speaker before. There are only two or so of the professors who have been outside Russia. Our contacts with the university also opened other doors. English teachers in schools in the city were eager to have us come and talk to their students, so we went to two secondary schools and one kindergarten. At the latter, we just said a few words to the children and I was asked by the Head Mistress to say a prayer with them, which I did. I think this was probably a breach of etiquette as far as the Orthodox Church is concerned. Ena visibly winced when one of the interpreters said, mistakenly, that I had "consecrated" the kindergarten, but I don't think it was the mistake in translation that was the point. It was that I had said a prayer with them. I think they probably see liturgical prayer as a priestly function. In the secondary schools we were very well received, given lavish meals, and gifts. The students as well as the teachers, again, are hungry for knowledge about the west. They look at you and they want to touch and get your autograph, etc.

They are also hungry about spiritual matters. Each time we spoke to the different groups of students and to the university classes about secular matters, they constantly injected questions about spiritual matters. The man who asked me to speak about British Christianity was a Muslim (Aslan).

It is evident that there is a great spiritual hunger in Russia today. This is apparent in almost every contact we had with individuals or groups. They were interested in the fact that I was a priest and looked to me and Peggy for some spiritual insight. This was true of Muslims as well as Christians. The Russian people have been bombarded with communist propaganda for almost 70 years. They have not been able to teach the faith or to worship without punishment, some of it severe, even death. The worshipping nucleus must be (although unfortunately we weren't able to make real contact with them) a very resolute and courageous group of believers. They have been through much and they are again a reminder of what Tertullian first wrote, that "the blood of martyrs is the seed of the church". The church has been shaped by the isolation of Russia from the European community and from European Christianity. In the communist years, as Ella pointed out, the church has had to draw into itself and look inward simply to protect the faith, much as the monastic communities protected the faith during the dark ages in Europe. So it has been shaped by the isolation of Russia and by communist persecution.

IV
Walkabouts and Visits

During the time the demonstrations went on, we were active every day. We moved from the hotel to an apartment provided by a man from the oil refinery, called the French House. There were no foreigners in Grozny except us and a group of Chinese. We had our own suite and we were able to have meals in the restaurant. The French House was considered a safe haven for us. We were told by Ludmilla that our suite cost £1.80/day. Fr. Piotr slipped Bill an envelope with 100 roubles. This was a slight embarrassment. Grozny didn't have a bank and we were unable to cash our travellers cheques. In a quiet evening, we figured we had enough in cash and £ notes to pay our hotel bill and 30p/day for food. But this was sufficient since almost all our needs were met by our many hosts.

The same afternoon Viktor, Ena and Fr. Sergei took us to visit three country parishes. Peggy wished she had a photo of me kissing one of the priests, a local custom and an honour. We had a meal at the last of the churches, sitting out of doors in the courtyard. The Church choir, consisting of about ten women and one older man, were building a new Church. Local Muslims had paid for the dome. The Choir also had prepared and served a bountiful meal, all home grown. Nothing was too good for the priest, Fr. Antoni. Because of fallout from the refinery, the tomato plants were sheltered and watered only with cow's milk. What would my father and grandfather have thought? They really believed oil was making the world a better place. They devoted their working lives to this. Fr. Antoni sat in the sunshine surrounded by his guests and parishioners. The choir even sang for us. It was a beautiful moment of peace in the midst of the turmoil. The next day we found the open market which I had visited as a boy. The shops had completely empty shelves but the market was full of autumn harvest.

Another day we went for a walk, looking for the post office. Tomisha recognized us as foreigners by our shoes. She invited us to visit her the next day. Sonia, Melika and Leila, students at the university, came along, and assured us it would be safe. We were told Chechins are very hospitable. Sasha, a part time journalist and university student, put an article about us in the local newspaper. People greeted us on the streets and asked us for autographs.

Father Piotr with Bill and Peggy, Ludmilla, Liza, Sergei and wife, Maya and Igor.

Visit to Village Church. Fr. Antoni with choir who were also building church and prepared meal.

Leila, Melika and Sonia.

Kindergarten.

The next day we went to visit an elite nursery, grouped by ages 3, 4, 5 and 6, subsidised by the oil industry. We were asked to lead the children in prayer in the classrooms. The children asked us: "Do English children like sweets and cartoons? Do you have grandchildren? Do you read them Russian fairy stories?" We had morning coffee and caviar with the Head Teacher. We were told that the staff at this nursery were paid more than the university lecturers.

Chechin Hospitality

We set out for Tomisha's, who seemed surprised to see us. Peggy had been worried about accepting an invite from a Chechin and her concern probably showed on her face, but Tomisha gave us lovely refreshments and invited us to return when her husband would be there. When we returned, husband Adam was there and we had another lovely meal, served by Tomisha who didn't sit with us until we asked Adam as a special favour for guests that he allow her to sit. He agreed readily. We discussed the deportations of the Chechins. Adam's brother Topa, the choreographer of the Chechin/Inguish Dance Company was there and he invited us to his home for another meal and also invited us to a dance rehearsal. They were preparing for a tour to South America. We didn't go to this because at the same time Adam and Tomisha invited us to go into the mountains to visit their home or tribal village.

The day came for the visit to Adam's home village. A large bus arrived with Tomisha and Mahmoud, the senior man, very much in charge. Another man, a

Tomisha's Party and Bus.

74

Imran, Peg and Helen – Picnic.

historian, gave a running commentary on the history of the area we passed through. We stopped at a mosque and were told that a Soviet bulldozer had come to knock down the mosque but God miraculously intervened and the bulldozer departed. We heard the same story about a Christian Church. As we went along we stopped every now and again and more people got on until the bus was full. When we got up into a mountain pass, we had to stop because the narrow road was being widened by blasting. We stopped at a beautiful mountainside overlooking a small river. Everybody piled out, the young men ran around cutting down saplings. I thought these Chechins had been in the city too long. You can't make a fire with green wood, but this wood was for the grid and shashlik (marinated lamb), which Tomisha had brought in a large tub. We also had cognac, tomatoes, bread, cucumbers, soup made from the lamb bones and chocolates. There was a very strict order of protocol. The senior man (in a hat) ate with Peggy and me, then the men in order of age, the senior woman, on down, to the children, who ate late.

There was plenty for all and we sat in the sunshine eating until it got dark. Once again, Paradise in the midst of conflict.

We visited Helen. Imran knocked on the door. They were an interesting pair who were good neighbours, he a young Muslin and she, middle aged Russian lecturer. He invited us to go out to the country in his car. Once again it didn't seem to bother anyone that our visas forbid this. But the KGB were kicked out, nitchevoo (no problem). Helen did say that it was safer to have one of them (a Chechin) with us. We brought some roses for Helen and she had prepared a small snack. But we kept stopping and Imran would go into a small shop and come back with packages. As it turned out, when he unpacked the boot he had an incredible amount of food (cheese, bread, tinned fish, salami, tomatoes, cabbage salad, shredded carrot, melons, grapes and apples, mineral water, lemonade and cognac). He also bought tables and chairs for our use. We stayed on the beautiful site until it got dark and then returned to Helen's flat. On our way, we were shown a white statue of a famous Chechin general which looked like the Red Army had used it for target practice. Did Helen and Imran survive?

Grozny University

We were asked to lecture at the University, Bill was asked to speak on English Parliamentary democracy, very much a live topic because Russia was searching for an alternative to communism. In the question period after the lecture on democracy, the first question was on God. God was the livelier topic after 70 years of atheism. Peggy lectured on education and British life, answering questions about wedding customs, prices and fashions. Later, Bill lectured on Church History. We had lunch with the faculty, with each contributing food. We were given more flowers. The University had a large faculty teaching English but only a few had been to Britain and most of their language came from tapes. One had a very posh Oxbridge accent.

Secondary School

We visited secondary schools and the pattern was the same. We would talk to the students and then would answer questions from both the teachers and students. At times we were asked to pray, and there were questions about Gorbachev and Yeltsin. One of the schools was an specialist scientific school for the elite and the best students academically. There were class privileges in the classless Soviet Union. We met with the students and then the teachers. They had a strong desire for us to talk about Christianity and we did. Fr. Piotr had given us permission to teach (we had some idea that this might happen). The teachers with the Principal came to us as we were leaving and pleaded us to stay on for a few weeks to teach religion. We had booked our flight and felt we should leave, for our own safety, if nothing else. It was hard but our courage was wearing a bit thin. The demonstrations were on the TV every night and it was anybody's guess where it was going. Our time had come. We tried to go back when we were selected as CMS Mission partners but CMS decided we were needed in Nigeria.

V

Grozny Revisited –
Personal Reminiscences

One of the purposes of the visit was to find, if possible, where we had lived in Grozny in 1939 and to see if anyone remembered me. I had my mother's letters written from Grozny to her parents and published in the local newspaper. This gave interesting information augmented by my own memories. What we didn't have was the actual address of the flat because the mail was addressed at that time to a post office box. I was able to locate the block of flats with reference to the boiler house that they had been building out in the middle of the complex and the proximity to the market. As a boy (1939) I took a photo of St. Michael and All Angels. One of the University students, Sasha, asked if he could do an interview. This appeared in the local newspaper and, as a part of the interview, people were asked to get in touch if they knew me in 1939-40. Unfortunately, the article didn't appear until we were nearly ready to leave. Nonetheless, we got together with one couple. They were brother and sister, the lady being several years older than I. They came to visit us in our lodgings in Grozny and we had an interesting conversation and then she took us to the flat. Her name was Aza. In 1939-40 she had known the previous American occupants of our flat, the Willises. She was particularly interested in making contact with Jerry Willis again. The reason the Willises left was that Mr. Willis had struck a Russian worker, and they had to leave in a hurry. She told me that Jerry Willis (the boy) had come over to their house the day after her father had been arrested and sent away to a concentration camp and said, accusingly, "I didn't know your father was a fascist, why didn't you tell me?" This must not have helped the family at that time. Her father was the Chairman of the Supreme Soviet of the Chechen-lngush Republic and he is remembered with a plaque on the wall of the flats across the street from where we lived. Aza identified the flat we had lived in (1939-40). It was No. 38, first floor corner with a long balcony. Later we went to the flat with the three friends (Leila, Sonia, Malika). A young woman in the back said it was her flat now, she invited us to go up to see it. It has been changed quite a bit since 1940 and made into a luxurious accommodation, but I was able to recognise the layout of the rooms. The old wood store/bathroom/

Brison Flats.

utility room has been made into a kitchen and a wall put across the former kitchen to make a second lounge. The block of flats has since been destroyed by Russian Army bombardment.

We were taken to the oil refinery where my father worked. The Oil Institute is important in Grozny, and they provided lodgings for us when we had to leave the Hotel Kabkas because of the revolution. Boris, who was helpful in obtaining the lodging and is quite high up in the Oil Institute, offered to take us to the refinery, but something happened and we never got there. Someone said that their husband was employed by the Oil Institute and they would look up the records and see if there was any record of my father having worked there. They reported back that the records did not go that far back. Tanta-

lizingly, there was an American who had married a Russian woman and stayed in Grozny who lived right across from where we lived. He died about five years ago. I wonder if he could have been a man named Rasmussen who was the only bachelor in the American group.

We had one other phone call in response to the newspaper article. It was a man who was at work during the day and could only come in the evening. His phone call came too late in our visit and we had no time free in the evening. This was too bad because he might have been nearer my age.

We thought it would be appropriate to throw a party on our last day (26 September) inviting as many as possible of our friends who had been generous and kind. We thought we had arranged a hot meal with the kitchen but Tanya came early and found they weren't prepared to cook. She went out and bought a lot of cold food. The guests helped prepare the meal. Fr. Piotr, Matusha Ludmilla, their granddaughter Liza, Tomisha, Lena, Tanya, Maya and her son, Maxim, Helen, Ella, Sasha and Viktor. Then they took us to the airport to fly to Moscow.

Grozny Oil Refinery built by Americans in 1939-40.

Farewell Party.

Chechnya Chronology

"An eye for an eye makes the whole world blind" Gandhi
The history of Russia/Soviets with Chechnya has been a seesaw of
brutality and revenge with massive innocent suffering
In the list below actions attributed to: Russians *Chechens*

1818 Czarist Russia invades and attempts to occupy Chechnya

1859 Chechen resistance ends with the capture of Chechen Muslin leader Shamil. Chechens immigrate to Armenia. Constant skirmishes from background of Tolstoy's novel, *The Cossacks.*

November 1920 Bolsheviks create Chechen Autonomous Province

1944 Stalin accuses Chechens of collaboration with advancing Nazi armies Red Army deports Chechen women and children to Kazakhstan

1957 Khrushchev allows survivors to return (50% had perished)

August 1991 General Dudayev (Red Army Chechen) coup topples Communists.

11th December 1994 Russian troops invade Grozny followed by 10 years of war Grozny destroyed, 100,000* civilian deaths

Father Piotr and Father Sergei taken hostage, presumed dead.

Baptist pastors' heads displayed in Grozny open market

Western workers heads impaled on stakes in Grozny outskirts

September 2004 Beslan School massacre, 171 Russian children, 30 terrorists die

In 2004, 386* Chechens abducted, 187 released, the rest missing or killed

3th and 28th December 2004 kidnapping* of two brothers, a sister, a niece and a nephew of Aslan Maskhadov, Chechen leader and former President

Over the years an estimated 30,000 Chechen children have been murdered.

**source Memorial, Russia's leading human rights group*

Going in hard with the guerrilla hunters of Chechnya

Eastern Battalion troops hold a 15-year-old boy during the Vedeno raid. They were looking for a man wanted for murder.

A Decade of War

December 1994: President Yelstin sends Russian troops into Chechnya to quash the independence movement

June 1995: Chechen rebels hold up to 2,000 hostages at a hospital in Budennovsk, South Russia. More than 100 die after botched commando raids

January 1996: Militants hold up to 3,000 people at a hospital in Kizlyar, Dagestan. The gunmen escape after a Russian attack, but more than 20 hostages are killed

September 1999: Bombs destroy apartment blocks in Moscow, Buynaksk and Volgodonsk, killing about 300 people. President Putin sends Russian troops back into Chechnya, blaming Chechen rebels

October 2002: 130 hostages and 41 Chechen terrorists die as Russian troops storm a Moscow theatre to end a siege

December 2002: 80 die in a bomb attack on a local government HQ in Grozny

May 2003: Suicide truck bombers kill 59 in a northern Chehnya government building

July 2003: Two women suicide bombers kill 15 at an open-air Moscow rock festival

August 2003: At least 50 die after a bomb-laden truck is crashed into a military hospital at Mozdok, North Ossetia

December 2003: An explosion on a commuter train on Russia's southern fringe kills 46

February 2004: A suicide bomber kills 39 on a Moscow underground train

May 2004: A bomb planted in a Grozny stadium kills the Kremlin-backed President Akhmad Kadyrov

August 2004: Two Russian passenger aircraft are blown up, possibly by suicide bombers, killing 89

September 2004: 330 hostages, mostly children, and 13 terrorists are killed after the Beslan school siege in North Ossetia

Acknowledgements

(Those who are dead or otherwise out of reach of the violence of those, on both sides, that this struggle has engendered)

1991 (unless otherwise noted)

The ten NGOs in Grozny whose heads were impaled on stakes on the Grozny city limits.

The Baptist pastors who were true to their namesake and had their heads displayed on platters in the Grozny open market.

Peggy and I might have been the first such martyrs except for the protection and hospitality afforded by:

The Grozny Orthodox Church of St. Michael and All Angels whose priests and congregation received us as a brother and sister in Christ, fed us, housed us and protected us. Their priest, Father Piotr and Father Sergei (his son) were taken hostage and haven't been heard of since. The Church building has been destroyed by Russian bombardment.

The people of Grozny, Chechen and Russian, who welcomed us joyfully, offered the hospitality of their homes, took us out into the countryside, offered us a safe house, at risk to themselves.

Viktor, Igor (ex. Red Army) and Ena, Grozny church people who met us and drove us around Grozny and the countryside.

The three young women, one Chechen, one Inguish, who befriended us. Are they alive? Did their friendship survive their holocaust?

The children of Beslan, wholly innocent victims of this brutal struggle.

The Orthodox Church in Moscow who put us up at no charge and shepherded us around and saw us on our way to St. Michael's, Grozny.

The Chechen communist Mayor of Grozny who in 1939 allowed his children to play with American children. He got the knock at the door in the middle of the night and disappeared for several years, his family ashamed of him for crimes he didn't commit.

The NKVD Commander (most likely) who in 1940 invited Billy Brison to his home and allowed his son to buy his $1.00 Mickey Mouse watch.

Yasha, interpreter and friend to the American community, who disappeared in 1940 after being suspected of listening to the BBC Overseas Service.

Robert Runcie, Archbishop of Canterbury, who gave our 1991 trip his blessing thus securing for us an entrée to the Russian Orthodox Church.

Josefina, Christian sculptress, aged 100, who showed us that if you have something to say a way can be found to say it.

386 Chechens abducted in 2004 in their own country, some dead, some still missing. The war goes on, the innocent still suffer.